GOD MEANT IT FOR GOOD

THE LIFE of JOSEPH

VOLUME 1

DR. DAVID JEREMIAH

with Dr. David Jeremiah

Contents

ABOUT
DR. DAVID JEREMIAH
AND TURNING POINT

D r. David Jeremiah is the founder of Turning Point, a ministry committed to providing Christians with sound Bible teaching relevant to today's changing times through radio and television broadcasts, audio series, books, and live events. Dr. Jeremiah's common-sense teaching on topics such as family, prayer, worship, angels, and biblical prophecy forms the foundation of Turning Point.

David and his wife, Donna, reside in El Cajon, California, where he serves as the senior pastor of Shadow Mountain Community Church. David and Donna have four children and twelve grandchildren.

In 1982, Dr. Jeremiah brought the same solid teaching to San Diego television that he shares weekly with his congregation. Shortly thereafter, Turning Point expanded its ministry to radio. Dr. Jeremiah's inspiring messages can now be heard worldwide on radio, television, and the Internet.

Because Dr. Jeremiah desires to know his listening audience, he travels nationwide holding ministry rallies and spiritual enrichment conferences that touch the hearts and lives of many people. According to Dr. Jeremiah, "At some point in time, everyone reaches a turning point; and for every person, that moment is unique, an experience to hold onto forever. There's so much changing in today's world that sometimes it's difficult to choose the right path. Turning Point offers people an understanding of God's Word as well as the opportunity to make a difference in their lives."

Dr. Jeremiah has authored numerous books, including *Escape the Coming Night* (Revelation), T*he Handwriting on the Wall* (Daniel), *Overcoming Loneliness, Grand Parenting, The Joy of Encouragement, Prayer—The Great Adventure, God in You* (Holy Spirit), *When Your World Falls Apart, Slaying the Giants in Your Life, My Heart's Desire, 31 Days to Happiness—Searching for Heaven on Earth, Captured by Grace, Grace Givers, Signs of Life, What in the World Is Going On?, The Coming Economic Armageddon, I Never Thought I'd See the Day!, God Loves You: He Always Has—He Always Will, What Are You Afraid Of?,* and *Agents of the Apocalypse.*

ABOUT THIS STUDY GUIDE

The purpose of this Turning Point study guide is to reinforce Dr. David Jeremiah's dynamic, in-depth teaching on the life of Joseph and to aid the reader in applying biblical truth to his or her daily life. This study guide is designed to be used in conjunction with Dr. Jeremiah's *God Meant it for Good—The Life of Joseph*, volume one audio series, but it may be used by itself for personal or group Bible study.

STRUCTURE OF THE LESSONS

Each lesson is based on one of the messages in the *God Meant it for Good—The Life of Joseph*, volume one audio series and focuses on specific passages in the Bible. Each lesson is composed of the following elements:

- *Outline*

The outline at the beginning of the lesson gives a clear, concise picture of the passage being studied and provides a helpful framework for readers as they listen to Dr. Jeremiah's teaching.

- *Overview*

The overview summarizes Dr. Jeremiah's teaching on the passage being studied in the lesson. Readers should refer to the biblical passages in their own Bibles as they study the overview.

- *Application*

This section contains a variety of questions designed to help readers dig deeper into the lesson and the Scriptures, and to apply the lesson to their daily lives. For Bible study groups or Sunday school classes, these questions will provide a springboard for group discussion and interaction.

- *Did You Know?*

This section presents a fascinating fact, historical note, or insight that adds a point of interest to the preceding lesson.

USING THIS GUIDE FOR GROUP STUDY

The lessons in this study guide are suitable for Sunday school classes, small-group studies, elective Bible studies, or home Bible study groups. Each person in the group should have his or her own study guide.

When possible, the study guide should be used with the corresponding compact disc series. You may wish to assign the study guide lesson as homework prior to the meeting of the group and then use the meeting time to listen to the CD and discuss the lesson.

FOR CONTINUING STUDY

For a complete listing of Dr. Jeremiah's materials for personal and group study call 1-800-947-1993, go online to www.DavidJeremiah.org, or write to: Turning Point, P.O. Box 3838, San Diego, CA 92163.

Dr. Jeremiah's *Turning Point* program is currently heard or viewed around the world on radio, television, and the Internet in English. *Momento Decisivo,* the Spanish translation of Dr. Jeremiah's messages, can be heard on radio in every Spanish speaking country in the world. The television broadcast is also broadcast by satellite throughout the Middle East with Arabic subtitles.

Contact Turning Point for radio and television program times and stations in your area. Or visit our website at www.DavidJeremiah.org.

GOD MEANT IT FOR GOOD

VOLUME 1

INTRODUCTION

When Walt Disney pioneered the production of animated films in the 1930s, each movie was labor intensive. Every second of film that was viewed on screen was the result of twenty-four individual drawings moving faster than the human eye could detect. Major movies like *Snow White and the Seven Dwarfs* required over one million individual drawings. Today, those drawings are done on computers—still labor intensive, but the computers do a lot of the laboring.

We look at a movie screen and see one image, not realizing that there are scores of individual images that our eyes can't detect. Our eye works at regular speed, while the film runs at "animator's speed."

That's how it is with God's providence in our lives. We see one "image" of life from our human perspective. It might be a troubling image we see or a wonderful one or a puzzling one. Our life is made up of individual moments, some of which we understand and some we don't, some of which we like and some we wish would quickly be over. But what we don't see are the other images that go together to create that impression of the world we see. God, like a constantly working artist, is drawing and compiling all the images we can't see that go together to produce what we can see.

We may see a major problem looming in front of us. But what we don't see are the rest of the images that represent God's work behind the scenes. There's the image of the reason, the image of the result, the image of the ramifications, short-term and long, and the image of the rest of our life. God is orchestrating all those images that we can't see to create the complete picture that someday we'll see and understand. Our challenge is to trust not only what our eyes see but what we don't see, to walk by faith and not by sight (2 Corinthians 5:7).

Joseph was a man who spent a lifetime trusting God with what he couldn't see. In this study guide, volume one of *God Meant It for Good*, you will meet the personification of trust in the providence of

God. From his days as a child, living in a family environment that was less than predictable or ideal, Joseph learned to believe that what he couldn't see was more important than what he could.

As a teenager, Joseph was sold into slavery by his own brothers. He landed in Egypt where he was purchased by an Egyptian official who ultimately put him in charge of all his affairs. He was then thrown into prison after being falsely accused of attacking the official's wife. In prison he was betrayed by a man for whose release he was responsible. And then when he was released, he was elevated to the second highest position of authority in all Egypt!

All the time Joseph was going from mountaintop to valley and back again, he never complained or questioned what God was doing. "Why Lord?" never passed through Joseph's lips. He had a unique spiritual ability to believe that God's hand was at work in every event in his life. God's providence in Joseph's life was never seen more clearly than when he had the opportunity to provide food and a place to live for his own father's family—even the eleven brothers who had sold him into slavery—as they traveled to Egypt to escape a famine in Canaan.

"God meant it for good" became Joseph's motto—his watch-word. And hopefully it will become yours as well as you study the life of a man who knew what it was to walk by faith and not by sight.

THE LIFE OF JOSEPH

Selected Scriptures

*In this lesson we survey the life of Joseph
as recorded in the book of Genesis.*

OUTLINE

Joseph is a major Old Testament character about whom nothing
negative is ever recorded in Scripture. He was a man who submitted
to the providential direction of God in his life and, in doing so, preserved the descendants of Jacob through whom the Redeemer of
man would come.

I. Joseph's Life Was Pivotal

II. Joseph's Life Was Providential

III. Joseph's Life Was Prosperous

IV. Joseph's Life Was Pure
    A. The Test of Self-Pity
    B. The Test of Sexual Enticement
    C. The Test of Self-Indulgence

V. Joseph's Life Was Prophetic

In every period of history, there are leaders and statesmen and women who stand out and are long remembered for various reasons. In the modern American era, President John F. Kennedy is one of those. Historians have long speculated on how America might have been different had he survived his first term and gone on to win a second. Instead, he was assassinated in the third year of his presidency.

John Kennedy was the youngest man ever to be elected president. Besides displaying the energy and appeal of a young man, he was handsome, wealthy, and had a beautiful wife. With such idealism was he viewed by many that his short term in Washington was called Camelot. He was the most popular president in the modern era.

A statesman in the Bible seems to have enjoyed the same level of popularity and charisma as did Kennedy—Joseph, the son of Jacob. Born into prominence in Canaan, he was sold into slavery in Egypt as a youth, but then rose to become the second most powerful man in the land. Both people of faith and those who study world literature recognize Joseph's story as one of the greatest in world history. His story has ambition, temptation, a poverty-to-palace theme, brilliance, wisdom, kindness, and high drama. He was certainly a leader who stood out in his day and has been remembered ever since.

Genesis is a book of biographies—the stories of its main characters. Following Adam, there are seven great men who walk through the pages of Genesis. Abel brought an excellent sacrifice to God, and Enoch "walked with God" and was taken up to heaven. Noah built an ark in obedience to God and preserved the human race. Next was Abraham, the friend of God, who defined what it meant to walk by faith. Next was Abraham's son, Isaac, who personified the submission of faith. Isaac's son, Jacob, was next—an up-and-down man who pictured what it was like to be in the school of faith. And finally there was Joseph, the favorite son of Jacob. It is his story that dominates the final chapters of Genesis. Joseph illustrates the success of faith— what it means to rise from tragedy to triumph by trusting in God.

Joseph's story is told from chapter 37 to chapter 50 of Genesis (excepting chapters 38 and 49 which touch on other subjects)—more of Genesis than is given to any of the other main characters. That fact alone is evidence of his importance in terms of Old Testament history. But once we begin to study Joseph's life, we discover many other worthwhile reasons to study him. He was a man whose faith was pivotal to his life and success.

JOSEPH'S LIFE WAS PIVOTAL

Joseph serves as a connector between the books of Genesis and Exodus—a hinge on which the story of the descendants of Abraham turns. If you don't know about Joseph, it's impossible to understand how Abraham's descendants go from being a family of shepherds in Canaan to a nation of over two million people in the Sinai wilderness.

After Joseph was sold into slavery as a teenager by his brothers, a famine came upon the land of Canaan and Egypt. Joseph had been elevated to a position of prominence in Egypt and was wise enough to have the nation store up grain for the seven years of famine. When his brothers came to Egypt looking for food to buy, they discovered the brother they had sold into slavery years before. After their tearful reunion, Joseph brought his father, Jacob, and all his family, seventy-two total (Genesis 46:27; Exodus 1:5; but see a different reckoning in Acts 7:14), to Egypt to escape the famine in Canaan. Pharaoh gave Joseph permission to settle his family in Goshen where they lived for 430 years (Exodus 12:40), increasing in number to more than two million souls: "So Israel dwelt in the land of Egypt, in the country of Goshen; and they had possessions there and grew and multiplied exceedingly" (Genesis 47:27). Had Joseph not been sent ahead to Egypt, there would have been no rescue for the descendants of Abraham.

In Exodus 1, we find a new pharaoh arising in Egypt who did not know Joseph. He feared that the rapidly multiplying Hebrews might gain too much power; so, while they were manageable, he subjected all of Jacob's descendants to slavery: "But the more [the Egyptians] afflicted [the Hebrews], the more they multiplied and grew. And [the Egyptians] were in dread of the children of Israel" (Exodus 1:12). No matter how they were afflicted, the Hebrew slaves continued to multiply, consistent with the promise of God to Abraham (Genesis 15:5; 22:17).

Joseph is the indispensable link between the seventy-two who entered Egypt and the two million who left.

JOSEPH'S LIFE WAS PROVIDENTIAL

When Teddy Roosevelt was campaigning for president in 1912, he was shot in the chest while delivering a speech. The bullet was deflected by a folded fifty-page speech and a metal glasses case that were in the inside pocket of his coat. The bullet lodged in his chest but did no permanent damage. Roosevelt later admitted that he had often complained about having to carry the heavy metal glasses case around, but admitted that it had saved his life.

What happened to Teddy Roosevelt was providential, and what happened to Joseph was providential as well, as he would ultimately confess. God took dark events in Joseph's life and used them to put him in a place by which he could save the descendants of Abraham from extinction during the famine in Canaan. Joseph's life is a perfect illustration of how God causes all things to work together for good "to those who love God, to those who are called according to His purpose" (Romans 8:28).

In Genesis 45, we find Joseph's brothers meeting him for the first time since selling him into slavery. They were terrified, thinking Joseph would exact revenge upon them for their former evil deed. But he tells them not to fear, that God had sent him to Egypt by their hands to prepare a way of deliverance for them (verses 5, 7). Joseph saw, and tried to convince his brothers, that God was at work in what they did. That didn't make their actions right, but God used their actions for good.

When their father Jacob died, the brothers thought again that Joseph would seek revenge. But Joseph told them that what they had meant for evil, God meant for good in order to save their family (Genesis 50:19–20). Joseph saw the big picture of what God had done. He saw that God's purposes were bigger than any man's plans. He saw that God could take a bad thing and turn it into a good thing. Joseph's story is the story of the providence of God.

JOSEPH'S LIFE WAS PROSPEROUS

I hear far too often that God is not interested in people succeeding—in winning at life. I hear Christian athletic coaches almost glorify losing because of all the lessons we can learn from it. I know from my own life that I don't need to work hard at losing because I am going to suffer losses naturally. It's just a part of life, and there are definitely lessons to be learned from the experience. But I believe it's totally appropriate for Christians to work hard at winning. Joseph was a winner. Indeed, it was his success that saved the descendants of Abraham from starvation.

Joseph's success can be followed by studying five dreams: two about himself while he was a teenager in Canaan, two from a butler and a baker while in prison in Egypt, and one dream of the pharaoh's that Joseph interpreted for him.

Joseph's two dreams about himself are found in Genesis 37:5–11. Both these dreams predicted Joseph's rise to prominence over his brothers and his family, and he might have been considered arrogant for relaying the dreams to his brothers. But he was just telling them what he saw; he believed the dreams were the message of God to him. He certainly didn't anticipate his brothers reacting so violently to the obvious message Joseph was communicating—his coming place of rule over his family.

But they did. One day they were in the field working when they saw Joseph approaching, and their sibling jealousy got the better of them. So they feigned Joseph's accidental death to their father and sold him to traders headed for Egypt. Years later when the brothers entered Egypt looking for food, they discovered Joseph's dreams had come true: He was the second most prosperous man in Egypt and held their very lives in his hand. Jacob's brothers, and ultimately Jacob himself, bowed down before Joseph just as his dreams had predicted. It was Joseph's predicted prosperity that saved his family's life.

Everything Joseph touched in Egypt turned to gold, figuratively speaking. He was a "successful man" (Genesis 39:2); "the Lord made all he did to prosper in his hand" (verse 3); "the blessing of the Lord was on all [Joseph] had in the house and in the field" (verse 5). Even when Joseph was falsely accused and thrown in prison, he prospered. He was put in charge of all the prisoners: ". . . and whatever he did, the Lord made it prosper" (Genesis 39:23).

It's important to note that Joseph didn't make himself prosper—it was the Lord who prospered him. Joseph was a winner and a success story worthy of study.

JOSEPH'S LIFE WAS PURE

It's interesting how God often has to send us the same message in life more than once before we get His point. Like a dog that returns to its vomit (Proverbs 26:11), so a fool repeats his folly. Even we who seek to follow the Lord don't always respond to God's reproofs the first time.

Joseph was no fool. He learned his lessons the first time, every time. Whenever God put Joseph in a potentially dangerous situation, he always took God's side. That meant he was promoted to the next level of test. There were three primary challenges in Joseph's life, all of which he passed with flying colors.

The Test of Self-Pity

Joseph had been persecuted by his own brothers, thrown into a pit, sold to slave traders, falsely accused and thrown into prison, and betrayed by a man in prison whom he helped to gain freedom. Joseph had a lot of reasons to feel sorry for himself and have his own pity party. But we do not find one word of self-pity or grumbling on Joseph's part from the beginning to the end of his story. He seemed to have the ability to see God and the good in every situation in life.

The Test of Sexual Enticement

When Joseph was falsely accused and thrown in prison, it was because he had resisted the sexual advances of his master's wife in Egypt. When Joseph resisted her seduction, she accused him to her husband of attacking her. It was his word against hers—in fact, she also had his coat that she pulled off him as he fled—and her word won the day. He declared two reasons for resisting her temptation: He refused to dishonor his master who had shown kindness to him, and he refused to dishonor God (Genesis 39:9). So Joseph passed the test of sexual temptation with flying colors and kept himself pure in the sight of God and man.

The Test of Self-Indulgence

Joseph's biggest test was when he was made ruler over all of Egypt, second only to the pharaoh in power and authority. The test was whether Joseph would use his power to enrich himself or use it to serve the people of Egypt. Predictably for him, he used it in the latter way. It was by his foresight and wisdom that he organized the nation to save enough grain in the good years to get them through the famine in the lean years. Passing the test of prosperity and power is often harder than passing the test of adversity. But Joseph passed successfully.

JOSEPH'S LIFE WAS PROPHETIC

I've already mentioned how the Bible records nothing negative about the life of Joseph. He is one of three of the major Old Testament characters about whom that is true, the other two being Daniel and Jonathan. Joseph's "perfect" record in the Old Testament makes him a prophetic illustration of the Lord Jesus Christ who was to come. A. W. Pink, a noted scholar of a prior generation, in his large commentary on the book of Genesis, lists a hundred similarities between the lives and ministries of Joseph and Jesus. Here are a few of the 100:

- Joseph was a shepherd feeding his sheep; Jesus said, "I am the good shepherd."
- Joseph was beloved of his father; God said of Jesus, "This is My beloved Son in whom I am well pleased."

- Joseph was hated by his brothers; Jesus said, "They hated Me without a cause."
- Joseph was not believed by his brothers; the New Testament says, "For even His brothers did not believe in Him."
- Joseph was envied by his brothers; and we read of Jesus, ". . . the chief priests had handed Him over because of envy."
- Joseph was sold for twenty pieces of silver; Jesus was sold for thirty pieces of silver.
- Joseph was sold into Egypt; and of our Lord we read, "Out of Egypt I called my Son."
- Joseph was a man in whom the Spirit of God was; and we read that God anointed Jesus with the Holy Ghost and with power.
- Joseph was put into a pit; Jesus was put into the grave.
- Joseph was taken out three days later; Christ came out of the grave on the third day.

The similarities are too numerous to be coincidental. In Joseph we have a prefiguring of Jesus Christ in whom true perfection was found.

A study of the life of Joseph will pay rich dividends for those who will take the time to mine the Scriptures concerning him. We should ask ourselves, Is my life a pivotal life? All of our choices impact other people—the question is, How? Are we looking for the evidence of God's providence in our lives? Do we trust before jumping to conclusions?

Are you asking God to make your life spiritually prosperous? Are you dreaming big dreams for God's kingdom? Too many of us are content with leaving a small footprint in the sand of life when we should be leaving a large one. You don't need to be a ruler over a nation to change this world, but you do need to have a world-changing dream.

And what about purity? Joseph remained faithful to God in a pagan culture, and we can too. And we do that by living faithfully for Christ, the ultimate personification of faithfulness in this world.

As we study Joseph together, may we be inspired by his life to change our world for Jesus Christ.

APPLICATION

From Genesis 37–50, answer the following survey questions about the life of Joseph:

1. How old was Joseph when he had his two dreams? (verse 37:2)

2. What did Joseph do that began to turn his brothers against him? (verse 37:2)

3. Describe Jacob's relationship with Joseph and his brothers' reaction to Jacob's favoritism. (verses 37:3–4)

4. Summarize Joseph's first dream and his brothers' reaction to it. (verses 37:5–8)

5. Summarize his second dream and the family's reaction. (verses 37:9–11)

6. How did Joseph end up in Egypt? (verses 37:12–28)

7. What lie did the brothers tell Jacob regarding Joseph's absence? How did Jacob respond? (verses 37:29–35)

8. The story of Joseph is interrupted in Genesis by the story of Judah and Tamar (Genesis 38). Read this story and see if you can find the reason Moses inserted this story here. (Look for clues in the later legislation given to Israel in Exodus 34:16, Deuteronomy 7:3, Joshua 23:12–13. What would likely have happened to the pure seed of Abraham had Jacob's family remained in Canaan?)

9. How would isolating Jacob's family in a protected environment allow them to maintain moral and physical purity as the promised line of blessing flowing from Abraham?

10. What was the feeling of Egyptians toward the Hebrews from Canaan when they arrived in Egypt? (verses 43:32; 46:34)

11. Where did the pharaoh settle the Hebrews? (verse 46:34) While the pharaoh thought he was protecting Egyptians from the "abomination" of the Hebrews, from what were the Hebrews being protected?

12. What event did God use to move Jacob's family into moral and spiritual protective care in Egypt? (verses 41:29–32; 56–57; 42:1–2)

13. So—why did Moses insert chapter 38 into the story of Joseph? What question was he answering for later generations?

14. How did Joseph summarize what God had done? (verses 50:19–21)
    Who did Joseph refer to with "many people"? (verse 20)
    In hindsight, who are the "many people" that were saved
    as a result of the Hebrews' isolation in Egypt for 430 years?

15. What do you learn about the extents to which God will go to
    preserve and protect those who are His?

16. How would you apply 2 Corinthians 6:14–18 on a spiritual
    level in light of how God separated Jacob's family from the
    temptations in Canaan?

17. Why should Christians not isolate themselves from the world?
    (Matthew 28:18–20)

18. What provision has God made to allow us to live in the world
    but not succumb to the world? (1 Corinthians 10:13; 1 John 4:4)

DID YOU KNOW?

There appears to be a biblical discrepancy in the descriptions
of the size of Jacob's family that left Canaan and sought refuge
in Egypt. Moses says the number was seventy (Genesis 46:27;
Exodus 1:5; Deuteronomy 10:22). However, in Stephen's speech
to the Sanhedrin in Acts 7, he says the number was seventy-five
(verse 14). The extra five arise from Stephen's use of the Septuagint,
the Greek version of the Old Testament. Genesis 46:20 in the
Septuagint includes the names of five sons and grandsons of
Joseph born to him in Egypt, taking the total from seventy to
seventy-five when added to the list of names of Jacob's family.

RISING ABOVE THE CIRCUMSTANCES

Genesis 37:1–11

In this lesson we discover that Joseph's circumstances were not an obstacle to his success in life.

OUTLINE

We live in a "no-fault" world. It's difficult to convince people today that they are responsible for their actions. It's much easier to blame society, parents, our childhood environment, or other circumstances. Joseph chose not to let circumstances limit his prospects for success.

I. Joseph's Hereditary Achievements
   A. Joseph Overcame Discord Among the Brothers
   B. Joseph Overcame Deaths in the Family
   C. Joseph Overcame His Honor in the Family

II. Joseph's Holy Life

III. Joseph's Heavenly Visions

IV. Our Responses
   A. Response of Humility
   B. Response of Honesty

In his book, *Competent to Counsel*, Christian counselor Jay Adams refers to Anna Russell's bit of humorous verse when he discusses Freudian psychotherapy —the idea that all our problems are a result of our heredity or environment:

> I went to my psychiatrist to be psychoanalyzed
> To find out why I killed the cat and blacked my husband's eyes.
> He laid me on a downy couch to see what he could find,
> And here is what he dredged up from my subconscious mind:
> When I was one, my mommie hid my dolly in a trunk,
> And so it follows naturally that I am always drunk.
> When I was two, I saw my father kiss the maid one day,
> And that is why I suffer now from kleptomania.
> At three, I had the feeling of ambivalence toward my brothers,
> And so it follows naturally I poison all my lovers.
> But I am happy; now I've learned the lesson this has taught;
> That everything I do that's wrong is someone else's fault.[1]

His point is that we live in an age in which people are quick to blame others for their problems; fewer people are willing to take responsibility for their own actions. From a study of Joseph's life, we learn that success is not dependent on circumstances, that anyone can rise above the limitations of their environment and succeed.

JOSEPH'S HEREDITARY ACHIEVEMENTS

While Joseph was part of the promised line of blessing flowing from Abraham, that did not mean he was raised in a perfect hereditary environment. Quite the contrary. Joseph's mother, Rachel, was an idolater (Genesis 31:19–20), and his father, Jacob, was a thief—he stole his brother's birthright. Jacob's rocky spiritual career is a fascinating spiritual story on its own.

Jacob was the grandson of Abraham, the son of Isaac, and the twin brother of Esau. The name "Jacob" meant "trickster" or "supplanter," and he seemed determined to live up to that name in the early years of his life. A study of Jacob is a study in the practice of deceit.

He began his career of deceit by tricking Esau out of his birthright, Esau being the firstborn of the two. Esau had been on a hunting trip and returned famished. Jacob offered him some of the stew he had prepared in exchange for his birthright. Jacob's motive was to receive the double-portion of their father's inheritance that would normally go to the firstborn. Foolishly, Esau agreed; and Jacob became the inheritor of the birthright of Esau.

When it was time for Isaac to die and bestow his blessing on his twin sons, Jacob further cemented the birthright he had stolen from Esau. With the help of his mother, Rebecca, they tricked Isaac, who was nearly blind at this point, into thinking that Jacob was Esau. When Isaac reached out to bestow the blessing of the firstborn on who he thought was Esau, he actually blessed Jacob instead. So Jacob cheated Esau a second time, the father's blessing being irrevocable.

When Esau discovered what had happened, he was so enraged that Rebecca sent Jacob into hiding with his uncle Laban. So Jacob traveled 450 miles away from Canaan to live with Laban in Haran. Laban was an even bigger crook and deceiver than Jacob was, and Jacob was about to get a taste of what it was like to be on the receiving end of trickery.

In Haran, Jacob fell madly in love with Laban's daughter, Rachel, and Laban promised Jacob he could have her in return for seven years of labor. Jacob agreed to the deal and worked for seven years to gain Rachel for his wife. But in Genesis 29, we discover that Laban double-crosses Jacob at the end of the seven years. On the night of his supposed marriage to Rachel, Laban brings Rachel's sister, Leah, to Jacob's tent and he lies with her, thereby consummating a marriage to Leah instead of Rachel. With Leah cloaked in the traditional veil that women wore in that day, Jacob didn't realize he was being given Leah instead of Rachel. The next morning, Jacob was furious with Laban, asking, "Why then have you deceived me?" (verse 25).

Jacob got a dose of his own medicine. He had worked seven years to win the hand of one woman, only to wake up the day after his wedding and discover he's been tricked into marrying a different woman. Laban had done to Jacob what Jacob had done to Esau—tricked him out of something that was rightfully his.

Even though he was now married to Leah, Jacob still wanted Rachel for his wife. Laban agreed to give Rachel to Jacob in exchange for another seven years of labor. Jacob finally got Rachel for his wife in addition to her sister Leah who was Jacob's first wife. Jacob was now married to two sisters, clearly a violation of God's creation ordinance of one man and one woman (Genesis 2). Wherever you find polygamy in the Old Testament, you find trouble.

That's the history of Joseph's parents—not ideal by any standard of righteousness.

Joseph Overcame Discord Among the Brothers

You can track Jacob's further exploits in Genesis until meeting him again in Genesis 37—the beginning of the story of Joseph where we find Joseph to be one of twelve sons born to Jacob and his wives. Joseph's brothers were very resentful of Joseph since he was the favorite son of Jacob (Genesis 37:4–5, 8). To understand the roots of this animosity toward Joseph, you have to look to the relationship between Jacob and his wives.

Leah bore Jacob four sons without problem: Reuben, Simeon, Levi, and Judah. But Rachel's womb was barren—she had given Jacob no children. In the Old Testament world, this was a disgraceful thing for a woman; so tension developed between the two wives of Jacob—one fruitful, the other not. Rachel and Jacob were at odds over the matter as well (Genesis 30:1–2).

Rachel decided to give her maid, Bilhah, to Jacob so she could bear children for Rachel as a surrogate. So two more sons were born from the union of Jacob and Bilhah: Dan and Naphtali. At this point, Leah had stopped bearing children so she decided to do what Rachel did. She gave Jacob her maid, Zilpah, and from that union came two more sons: Gad and Asher. So now there are four sons from Leah, two sons from Rachel's maid, and two sons from Leah's maid.

One day when Leah's oldest son, Reuben, was in the fields, he discovered a rare mandrake plant, believed to promote fertility in women in ancient cultures. When he brought them home to his mother, Rachel found out about it and asked Leah to share her mandrakes with her; but Leah refused (Genesis 30:15). Since Leah had not been with Jacob in a long while, Rachel offered her the chance to sleep with Jacob in exchange for the mandrakes. But she got more than she bargained for. Leah bore Jacob two more sons: Issachar and Zebulun. So now the count is up to ten sons between the wives and maids—and Joseph still hadn't been born.

After all Rachel's efforts—her own, her maid's, the mandrakes—God "listened to [Rachel] and opened her womb" (Genesis 30:22). I recall a dear elderly woman who prayed for my wife when we were unable to have children early in our marriage. Finally, my wife became pregnant, and I called her up and told her she could stop praying! It is the Lord who opens and closes the womb, and that was the case with Rachel.

The first child Rachel bore to Jacob was a son whom they named Joseph. Not long after, a second son was born named Benjamin. With the addition of a daughter born to Leah, named Dinah, the household of Jacob was complete: twelve boys and one girl. Surveying how the twelve sons were born—the tension, the jealousy, the jockeying for position—it's no wonder that there was tension among them. And especially toward Joseph: remember—Joseph was the firstborn son of the love of Jacob's life, Rachel. For that reason, he was the favored son of all the twelve to Jacob.

Joseph Overcame Deaths in the Family

There were three deaths in Joseph's family when he was growing up, all of which had an effect on him. First, Deborah, the maid of Isaac's wife, Rebekah (Genesis 24:59; 35:8), died. Deborah had become attached to Jacob's family; and when she died, Jacob's family named the tree under which she was buried *Allon Bachuth*—possibly "the oak of weeping." We know little about her, but she must have been like an elderly grandmother to Jacob's young sons.

Not long after, Joseph's grandfather Isaac died. In Genesis 35, we see that Jacob helped to bury Isaac in the cave of Machpelah where Abraham and Sarah were buried and where Jacob would also be buried in time.

As moving as those two deaths must have been for Joseph, the third was the one that broke his heart: the death of his mother, Rachel. Sixteen years had passed between the birth of Joseph, the eleventh son, and Benjamin, the twelfth. In giving birth to Benjamin, Rachel died.

Joseph Overcame His Honor in the Family

So Joseph was a man who grew up in a very complicated household and who experienced several painful separations. In other words, his upbringing was "normal" in the sense that it wasn't perfect. And add to that the jealousy of his brothers toward him. While showing favoritism to children is not advisable, it's easy to understand why Jacob was partial to Joseph. Every time he saw Joseph's face as a young man, he saw the face of his beloved Rachel. Joseph was the son of the woman for whom he had labored faithfully for fourteen years. Jacob was probably more like a grandfather than a father to Joseph, treating him favorably as grandfathers are wont to do. The coat of many colors Jacob gave Joseph was an indication of his favoritism and affection—and another reason for his brothers' jealousy (Genesis 37:3–4). The coat was a symbol to the other sons that Joseph was destined to be the favored heir of their father.

Reuben was actually the firstborn of Jacob (from Leah), but we learn from 1 Chronicles 5:1 why he didn't receive that inheritance: Reuben had defiled his father's bed, and the right eventually passed to the sons of Joseph. (Reuben slept with one of his father's concubines— a seriously immoral and disrespectful act; Genesis 35:22; 49:4.) The right of the firstborn passed down the line to Joseph since he was the firstborn of Jacob's other legitimate wife, Rachel. No doubt the sons who were skipped over were resentful of the blessing jumping down the family tree to Joseph, though it was correct that it should.

This was a family full of twists and turns that could have turned Joseph bitter toward God and others. But he somehow did not let his heredity nor his circumstances ruin him.

JOSEPH'S HOLY LIFE

Joseph, at age 17, had seen the sons of Bilhah and Zilpah (his brothers Dan, Naphtali, Gad, and Asher) doing something he knew would bring a reproach upon his father's name (Genesis 37:2). So he went to Jacob and reported to him his brothers' actions. While we don't know what they were doing, it was apparently serious enough (as indicated by the phrase "bad report") to warrant Joseph bringing it to Jacob's attention. Rather than just being a tattletale, the impression from Scripture is that Joseph was concerned for his father's and God's reputations.

Joseph's brothers were a dangerous lot. They once had murdered an entire village in retaliation for their having defiled their sister, Dinah. But Joseph was not part of that retaliatory action. He had a righteous heart, and we find him separated from his brothers in that way. Holiness always brings jealousy and envy from those who are unholy, and it turned out to be true in Joseph's case. While he shouldn't have been persecuted for being holy, it was just one more thing his brothers didn't like about him.

JOSEPH'S HEAVENLY VISIONS

We find in the early part of Genesis 37 the two dreams that Joseph had and ultimately shared with his brothers. The dreams were an obvious indication that he would one day be in a place of superiority over his brothers and parents. Whether Joseph should have shared the dreams with his brothers is a matter of debate that is hard to decide. But we do know this: The dreams painted a picture of history that ultimately was perfectly fulfilled in Joseph's life. But before that scenario became real, Joseph's brothers were incensed (as was his father Jacob) at what they perceived to be Joseph's arrogance and self-promotion.

No one, including Joseph, knew how the dreams would be fulfilled at the time Joseph had them. But everyone ultimately realized the dreams were from God. The effect of the dreams when Joseph was a teenager was to turn his brothers even more vehemently against him. Joseph had a sense of purpose and destiny about his life that his brothers greatly resented.

It's always true that people who know where they are headed in life will receive opposition from those who are lost. People who are in touch with God and walking confidently and faithfully with Him will not be welcomed by those who are not.

Our Responses

It's obvious that Joseph was not raised in a perfect environment. Even so, he never blamed his family or heredity when he landed in a pit in Canaan or a prison in Egypt. He just continued to trust God. What can we learn from his outlook and actions?

Response of Humility

First, we ought to be humbly thankful to God for the positive circumstances in which most of us were raised and which we enjoy in our lives. Life has been very difficult for some, but for most Americans, compared to the rest of the world, life has been very prosperous. When we think life is treating us badly, we ought to remember Joseph, how he never blamed God or anyone else for his troubles.

Response of Honesty

Second, we need to be honest. If we have experienced negative influences or events in our lives, we are still responsible for our response to those negative circumstances. Ultimately, our lives are not dictated to us by others; our lives are what we have chosen them to be. Yes, prior events in our lives can make the right choices more challenging. But with God's help, we can choose to succeed just like Joseph did. We can have our dreams and vision for our lives and fulfill them by the grace of God if we will choose not to be disabled by people and circumstances.

May you choose to be like Joseph in your generation.

Notes:

1. Jay Adams, *Competent to Counsel: Introduction to Nouthetic Counseling* (Grand Rapids: Zondervan, 2009), 8.

1. From Genesis 31:38–42, describe the 20 years that Jacob spent in service to Laban. What were the purposes? What positive attributes of character can you find in Jacob's history with Laban?

2. How did Jacob's name get changed to Israel, and why? How did Israel commemorate the event? (Genesis 32:22–32; 35:9–10)

3. Describe the reunion between Jacob and Esau, the estranged brothers. What do you find commendable in Jacob's (Genesis 33:3) and Esau's (verse 4) actions?

4. From Genesis 35:23–26; 35:16–18, make a list of the children born to Jacob's wives and their maids:

Leah	Rachel	Bilhah (Rachel's maid)
1.	1.	1.
2.	2.	2.
3.		
4.		Zilpah (Leah's maid)
		1.
5.		
		2.
6.		
7.		

5. What promises did God make to Jacob at Bethel?
   (Genesis 35:11–13)

   a. Regarding descendants: (verse 11)

   b. Regarding land: (verse 12)

6. What was in danger of happening to Jacob's descendants?
   (Genesis 34:8–10; 38:1–7)

7. Esau's descendants populated today's modern Arab nations
   (Genesis 36). To whom did God promise the land of Canaan?
   (Genesis 35:12)

   a. What did Esau voluntarily do in terms of occupying that
      same land? (Genesis 36:6–8)

   b. That left the descendants of Jacob to occupy the promised
      land of Canaan and the descendants of Esau to populate
      the surrounding lands. How has this arrangement deterio-
      rated as evidenced by today's geopolitical tensions in the
      Middle East?

8. What is there in Joseph's words in Genesis 37:7 that likely would have infuriated his brothers?

a. Who did the sun, moon, and stars represent in the second dream? (verse 9)

b. Why do you think Jacob "kept the matter in mind"? (verse 11)

c. What similar response do you find in Mary, the mother of Jesus? (Luke 2:19, 51)

d. How does James 1:19 figure into these kinds of situations—when someone says something we don't understand?

e. Based on what you've learned about Joseph, why do you think he told his brothers and father about his dreams?

f. Would you have advised him to reveal the dreams or not? Why?

g. Given the level of integrity we find in Joseph's life, how might he have been justified in revealing the dreams?

9. What limitations or negative experiences in your own life have you experienced?

a. To what degree do you feel they have "held you back"?

b. What have you learned from this lesson about the need to take responsibility for moving beyond limiting circumstances?

DID YOU KNOW?

Everyone is familiar with traditional images of Joseph's "tunic of many colors" given him by his father Jacob (Genesis 37:3). The coat is usually pictured as a modern bathrobe-type garment consisting of vertical, rainbow-hued stripes. In reality, Joseph's coat was more likely a long, white, ankle-length, long-sleeved tunic. Around the hem of the sleeves and the hem of the tunic would have been a colored, or multi-colored ribbon accenting the white. Joseph's tunic would have stood out from his brothers' dramatically. Theirs would have been short sleeved and not ankle length, made from a rougher material with no color—a typical "workingman's" garment of the day. Joseph's tunic would have set him apart as the preeminent son among the twelve sons.

JOSEPH'S FATHER

Genesis 28–35

In this lesson we learn what it took for Jacob to surrender to God's will for his life.

OUTLINE

An old saying is often heard: "We can do this the hard way or the easy way." Jacob chose the hard way. God intended to bless Jacob, but he wasn't willing to wait for God's time and place. By forging ahead in his own strength, Jacob didn't come to know God until near the end of his life.

I. **Jacob's Four Crises**
   A. The Crisis at Bethel
   B. The Crisis at Peniel
   C. The Crisis at Succoth
   D. The Crisis at Bethel

II. **Jacob's Life Lessons for Us**
   A. God Will Not Spare Present Pain if It Means Eternal Profit
   B. God Will Persevere When We Have Given Up on Ourselves and on Him
   C. God's Priority for Your Life Does Not Include a Jacob Experience

J oseph's father was Jacob, a man who might fit the mold of the modern American macho-male—the guy who finagles himself to the top by hook or by crook and leaves a trail of dead and wounded bodies behind him. Jacob was shrewd and crafty, willing to do whatever it took to accomplish his goal. Success was everything to Jacob.

We criticize his methods while sometimes forgetting that God had prophesied Jacob's success. In Genesis 25:23, when Jacob and his twin brother were being born, God said, "One people shall be stronger than the other, and the older [Esau] shall serve the younger [Jacob]." God predicted that Jacob would be the leader among the two, and he was. The problem with Jacob was the methods he used to achieve the success God had promised.

Deep down, Jacob seemed to have a genuine desire and capacity for spiritual things, but he kept sabotaging that capacity by his carnal actions. G. Campbell Morgan, a great Bible commentator, wrote that Jacob desired the blessing of his father Isaac, but his fear secured it by trickery. Faith desired the birthright that was his by divine arrangement, but fear secured it by meanness and deceit.

Four things happened as a result of Jacob's trying to make something happen instead of waiting on God to bring it about:

> First, Isaac, Jacob's father, got what he deserved. Isaac was a weakling who loved his outdoorsman son Esau for the wrong reasons and blessed Jacob for the wrong reasons. He earned the turmoil he experienced.
>
> Second, Esau got what he deserved, giving up his birthright for a bowl of stew and piece of bread! His priorities were obviously misplaced.
>
> Third, Jacob was forced to spend 20 years in exile as a result of his deceiving ways and unwillingness to trust God's timing and plan.
>
> And fourth, Rebekah lost the son she loved most. By helping Jacob be deceitful, she never saw him again after he fled for his life from Esau.

All of the members of this family reaped what they sowed.

JACOB'S FOUR CRISES

In this lesson we'll study Jacob's life in terms of four major crises he experienced. By way of background, Jacob was told by his mother

Rebekah to flee from Esau's wrath by going to Haran and staying with Laban, Rebekah's brother, until it was safe to return—a trip of 450 miles that lasted twenty years.

The Crisis at Bethel

On his way to Haran, Jacob stopped to sleep at a place called Luz. While sleeping, he had a dream in which God spoke to him and confirmed that he would inherit the promises made to Abraham and Isaac (Genesis 28:13–15). Jacob was so overwhelmed by this revelation that he created a monument to the Lord and named the place Bethel or "house of God." But true to his nature, the first thing Jacob did was to try to make a deal with God: Bless me and I will repay a tenth of all You give me (verses 20–22).

I believe this was a self-centered vow on Jacob's part, an attempt to use God to further his own interests. Jacob had not changed at this point, having just come from committing major acts of deceit to get what he wanted. But who among us would say that we have never approached God that way in our own life: "Lord, if You'll do so-and-so, I'll repay You by doing so-and-so."

The good thing about vows is that you can test their genuineness by seeing if they were ever fulfilled. After having studied the life of Jacob thoroughly, I can't find any evidence that, over the next twenty years, Jacob was serious about the vow (or "deal") he proposed to God. All the years he spent in Haran seemed to be self-centered, not God-centered. Getting a wife and increasing the size of his flocks and herds seemed to be his highest priority. If he thought of God at all, it was probably in terms of how God could help him, not how he could serve God.

Jacob was a confirmed materialist. As the vision of his own prosperity increased, the memory of his Bethel experience grew smaller.

The Crisis at Peniel

After twenty years at Haran, Jacob finally decided to return to Canaan. He was a hundred years old (he lived to be 147; Genesis 47:28), so he was in his prime. He had a family, huge herds, abundant servants and resources, and had seen enough swindling in his life—his and others'—to last a lifetime. But just as he had an encounter with God leaving home, he had another encounter with God as he returned home (Genesis 32:1–12).

As Jacob approached the land of Edom where Esau dwelt, he sent messengers ahead to assess the situation. They returned saying that Esau was coming to meet Jacob with a force of 400 men—so the schemer devised a plan. He divided his entire company of family, servants, and animals into two groups, believing that if Esau attacked one, the other might escape. And then he miraculously remembered the promise God made to him more than two decades ago: "Deliver me, I pray . . . . For You said, 'I will surely treat you well . . .'" (verse 12; see 28:13–15). Now that Jacob is in trouble, he finds it convenient to remember God's promise to prosper and protect him.

So Jacob sent his servants with presents to Esau and sent his wives, eleven sons, servants and animals on ahead. Left alone, that night Jacob once again encountered God.

1. Dealing With Strong, Self-Willed People

What happens to Jacob makes a good outline for how God deals with self-willed people (which includes all of us at some point in our lives).

a. Human Solitude

Genesis 32:24 says, "Then Jacob was left alone . . . ." Little by little God knocks the support system out from under strong-willed people so they are left with nothing but themselves and God. Jacob had no one to manipulate or work a deal with. His hands were tied.

b. Divine Discipline

Next came discipline: ". . . and a Man wrestled with him until the breaking of day" (verse 24). "Man" is capitalized in our English Bibles because this was a theophany—a manifestation of God Himself. Jacob didn't wrestle with this Man; rather "a Man wrestled with him." God was working on Jacob to break down his defenses and his self-confidence. It is a terrible thing to be hammered on by God because we won't yield to His will, but God will do whatever it takes.

c. Human Opposition

Jacob was strong—he resisted God's discipline throughout the night. Self-willed people don't give up easily, which makes the process of discipline all the more difficult. The more we resist, the harder God works to break our stubborn will. God touched "the socket of his hip" and put it out of joint (verse 25), giving Jacob a permanent limp as a reminder of their encounter. I have read that "the sinew of the hip" (the literal translation) is the strongest part of the human body, able to be broken only by twisting it. So God twisted Jacob until he was made lame, and his self-will was broken. God broke Jacob's strength and made him weak and dependent.

In verse 26 there is a change in Jacob. Instead of resisting God as before, now he is clinging to God, refusing to let Him depart without giving him a blessing: "I will not let You go unless You bless me!" Jacob is hanging on to God for dear life. He has been transformed from someone who is cunning to someone who is clinging; from someone who is resisting to someone who is resting; from someone who is crafty to someone who is conquered.

Finally, Jacob was broken, and God was willing to bless him. By asking Jacob his name, God got him to admit who he was: a trickster (verse 27).

2. Result of Struggle

As a result of his confrontation with God, Jacob got a new character and a new name.

a. New Character

God wanted to have a close, blessed relationship with Jacob all along. He wanted Jacob to be a man of God, not a man among men. And finally, that is what Jacob became. He became a man who was willing to do God's will instead of his own. His character was transformed from being a deceiver of men to being a servant of God.

Satan tests us where we are weakest in order to destroy us, while God tests us where we are strongest in order to employ us. Jacob was now ready to be "strong in the Lord and in the power of His might" (Ephesians 6:10). God didn't wound Jacob to make him weak, but to make him stronger, much as Paul became stronger in the Lord by his thorn in the flesh (2 Corinthians 12:7–10). God gave Jacob time to surrender willingly; but when he didn't, God forced the issue.

b. Name Changed

Jacob also got a new name: Israel (Genesis 32:28). "Israel" means "prince of God," which is who God wanted Jacob to be all along. And it's who God wants us to be as well—someone who is blessed by God and enjoys an intimate relationship with Him.

Even though Jacob went through a true conversion at Peniel, he still experienced relapses (which should be an encouragement to us). That leads us to the third and fourth crises in Jacob's life.

The Crisis at Succoth

When Jacob and Esau finally met, they made peace with one another. Esau invited Jacob to journey with him back to their homeland (Genesis 33:12). But Jacob created an excuse to send Esau on ahead while he continued the journey slowly with his family and flocks. He told Esau he would meet him in Seir—but he was lying (verse 14)! He was back to his old ways just days after his encounter with God. Instead of going to Seir to be reunited with his brother, Jacob went to Succoth and settled his family there. He had feigned submission to Esau to keep from being killed; but when he found out Esau had forgiven him, he was ready to do his own thing again.

Jacob eventually moved on to Shechem and settled there— which set the stage for Jacob's sons murdering the residents of Shechem when they violated Jacob's daughter, Dinah (Genesis 34). Had Jacob done what he should have done—returned to Seir with his brother—that terrible tragedy never would have occurred.

The Crisis at Bethel

God continues to work with Jacob, telling him to move back to Bethel where He first appeared to Jacob when he was fleeing from Esau (Genesis 35:1). Jacob's family buried all their idols in the ground, and they built an altar and worshiped God, naming the place "God of the house of God" (El Bethel). God had taken precedence in Jacob's mind.

Jacob never again reverted to his scheming ways. He had fought with God for his whole life and was now ready to live in harmony with Him.

JACOB'S LIFE LESSONS FOR US

There are three lessons we can learn from Jacob's life (since there is some of Jacob in all of us).

God Will Not Spare Present Pain if It Means Eternal Profit

God is more concerned about our spiritual growth than our temporal comfort. And often we are concerned with just the opposite. Listen to the prayers often heard when Christians gather to pray: "Give us a good week . . . . Give us the money we need . . . . Help us get a good job . . . . Help our children succeed . . . . Keep us healthy . . . . Help our church to grow . . . ." Sometimes we get the mistaken idea that God's job is to make our life comfortable and successful.

While God does bless us with many things that we pray for, our comfort is not His top priority. Instead, God wants us to be righteous; to be spiritually mature. When dealing with Jacob, God did not spare the pain to get him to a place of submission and responsibility. Many of the things God allows in our lives are designed to make us uncomfortable in order that we might become submissive to Him.

God Will Persevere When We Have Given Up on Ourselves and on Him

The principle of Philippians 1:6 and 1 Thessalonians 5:24 is in view here: What God starts, He will finish! God doesn't give up on us regardless of how long it takes us to put Him first in our lives.

It's amazing to me that God refers to Himself, and allows others to refer to Him, as "the God of Jacob" (Exodus 3:6, 15; 4:5; 2 Samuel 23:1; Psalm 20:1; 46:7, 11; 75:9; 81:1, 4; 94:7; 114:7; 146:5 and more). He even says in Malachi 1:2, "Yet Jacob I have loved" (Romans 9:13). Instead of being embarrassed by Jacob, God declares Himself the God of Jacob even though Jacob resisted Him most of his life.

If you are running from God right now, be aware that He is not running from you. If you look over your spiritual shoulder, you will likely see Him in pursuit, gaining ground on your heart and soul. You may have given up on you, but God has not.

God's Priority for Your Life Does Not Include a Jacob Experience

It's not up to us to ignore God in our lives so that God can be faithful to come and find us. That is not the message of this lesson at all. God doesn't want our life to include a "Jacob" experience. Instead, he wants us to submit to Him at the beginning and allow Him to work out His plan steadily throughout our lives.

Look at the difference between Jacob's life and his son Joseph's life. God intended to bless Jacob from the day of his birth, but Jacob set out to make it happen himself and ruined most of his life. Joseph, on the other hand, was given dreams by God that he was going to be blessed and immediately found himself in a pit and on his way to Egypt as a slave. But Joseph submitted to that process—he stayed faithful to God and let God work it out His own way. And sure enough, Joseph was elevated and blessed at the beginning of his life while Jacob didn't get blessed until near the end of his life.

I recommend you seek a Joseph experience and not a Jacob experience in your life. The sooner you let God have His way with you, the sooner you will begin to experience His blessing and know His success. The alternative may turn out to be uncomfortable: wrestling with God.

APPLICATION

1. How old was Jacob when he arrived in Egypt with his family to escape the famine? (Genesis 47:9)

    a. How did Jacob describe his life to the pharaoh? (verse 9)

    b. Based on what you learned about Jacob in this lesson, how accurate was his assessment of his life?

    c. Do Jacob's words in verse 9 sound like a humbled and converted man or a man still going his own way?

    d. Do you detect sorrow in his words? If so, why? What sorrow is shared by those who reject God's offers once they have a change of heart?

    e. At what age do you think most people become Christians? (youth, young adult, middle-age, elderly?) Why is it harder to be converted the older one gets?

    f. What motivation do you find in Jacob's life to "redeem the time"? (Ephesians 5:16; see also Psalm 90:12)

    g. What regrets, if any, do you have about the point in life at which you submitted yourself to the Lord?

2. Read Genesis 25:21–34.

   a. What unusual experience did Rebekah have when she was pregnant with Esau and Jacob? (verse 22)

   b. What explanation did God give her about the situation? (verse 23) What did the plural "peoples" imply?

   c. Who was "the older" and who was "the younger" of the twins? (verses 25–26)

   d. Whose "people" would ultimately serve the other?

   e. If Esau's modern descendants are the Arabs and Jacob's are the Jews, how would you apply verse 23 to the tension between the two in our day? Based on verse 23, what would you anticipate the outcome of their struggle to be?

   f. How were the boys different? How were they viewed by their parents? (verses 27–28)

g. As the firstborn, Esau held the birthright. How did he lose it? (verses 29–33)

h. How would you characterize Esau's priorities based on this encounter? And Jacob's?

i. Why is impulsiveness a dangerous trait? How does Proverbs 25:28 describe what happened to Esau?

j. How does the last phrase of verse 23 indicate God's plan for Jacob's preeminence over Esau? How do you think God might have transferred the birthright from Esau to Jacob?

k. Describe a time in your life when you moved ahead of God instead of waiting on His perfect timing to transpire.

3. How were Jacob's grandfather Abraham (Genesis 12:10–20) and his father Isaac (Genesis 26:1–11) also guilty of deception?

DID YOU KNOW?

The name "Jacob" in Hebrew (*Yaaqob*) was derived from a Hebrew root word (*aqeb*) meaning heel, footprint, or hind part. The verb form could mean "to follow on the heel" or "attack from close behind" or "overreach." To "give someone the heel" meant to take advantage of him. As a name, *Yaaqob* was doubly significant for Jacob. When he was born, he came out grasping his twin brother Esau by the heel, "so his name was called Jacob" (Genesis 25:26). As a man, the figurative meaning of *Yaaqob* fit Jacob well as he was known to be quick to take advantage of others.

BETRAYED BY HIS BROTHERS

Genesis 37:12–26

*In this lesson we see the power of envy
to destroy lives.*

OUTLINE

It is a natural reaction, when hearing a message that makes us uncomfortable, to shoot the messenger. That's what Joseph's brothers did. They didn't like his message that he would one day rule over them, so they got rid of him. But God preserved the message and the messenger.

I. Jacob's Request
A. The Place
B. Past Performance

II. Joseph's Response
A. Courageous Obedience
B. Complete Obedience

III. Brothers' Reception
A. The Brothers' Plot
B. Reuben's Proposal
C. Judah's Plan
D. Reuben's Panic

IV. The False Report
A. Purposeful Deception
B. Jacob's Remorse

V. Believer's Response
A. The Power of Envy
B. The Pretense of Morality
C. The Penalty of Sin
D. The Providence of God

Life's abrupt and unexpected changes are always difficult, but they're all the more challenging when you're in the seventh grade.

When I was that age, my father gathered our family around the kitchen table one night and told us we would soon be moving from Dayton, Ohio, to the much smaller town of Cedarville. He had been asked to leave his pastorate and accept the presidency of a small Christian college with ninety students and no money, called Cedarville College. And he had said yes.

I thought my world had come to an end. I had just begun to develop my long-anticipated football career in the local Boy's Club football program, and I was just sure I was destined for the NFL. The day after my father's announcement, I found out Cedarville didn't even have a boys' football program. Someone had gotten killed playing football there a few years earlier, and they had cancelled the program.

I realize now that what I thought was the darkest day of my young life was a day God would use significantly in my life in the years to come. It was in Cedarville—living there and as a student in the college—that I learned some of the most important faith lessons of my life. The opportunity to watch my dad's leadership skills as he grew a struggling college into an institution with a significant impact in the Midwest was invaluable.

It was in Cedarville that I substituted basketball for football, something that paid my way through college. It was in Cedarville that I met and fell in love with Donna Thompson, who became my wife. It was there that I got exposed to broadcast ministry by working as a disc jockey at the college radio station. And it was there that my heart became burdened for ministry as I watched young men leave to become pastors, and as I listened to a constant stream of visiting Christian leaders, teachers, and missionaries who came to speak on campus.

Looking back, moving to Cedarville was a great move. But on that day in the seventh grade, I thought moving to Cedarville was like moving to the ends of the earth.

Everyone has times when they cry out to the Lord, "What are You doing?" When we can only see the first step in a journey, we resent having to go. And that must surely be how Joseph felt when his brothers' actions resulted in his being sold into slavery in Egypt. But it is from Joseph that we learn that God is always in control of our lives.

JACOB'S REQUEST

Genesis 37 is where Joseph's dark day begins. His life had been bright to that point—the favored son of his father who had become wealthy during twenty years in Haran (Genesis 30:43). The darkest day of his life was probably the day his mother Rachel died (Genesis 35:16–20), after which time Jacob settled with his twelve sons and one daughter in Hebron.

The Place

Jacob had sent the ten older boys to graze the flocks in Shechem, and Joseph was sent to check on them. It's no wonder Jacob was concerned about his sons since Shechem was the place where his sons Simeon and Levi had slaughtered all the males of the city in retaliation for their abuse of Dinah, Jacob's daughter (Genesis 34).

Past Performance

Jacob's sons were a rough lot, not averse to evil activity (Genesis 37:2). So Jacob wanted to check up on them and see how they were doing.

JOSEPH'S RESPONSE

When Joseph arrived in Shechem, the brothers were not to be found. Asking a local man for help, Joseph discovered the brothers had moved on to Dothan to graze the flocks. So Joseph went and found them there.

Two things can be noted about Joseph that set him apart from his brothers—two different aspects of obedience.

Courageous Obedience

Joseph knew he wasn't popular with his brothers; so when his father told him to journey alone to check on them, it took courage to obey. Whatever apprehension he might have felt about his brothers' impulsiveness and volatility was well-founded as he was soon to discover. Regardless, without a word, he obeyed his father's request.

Complete Obedience

Joseph was responsible enough to complete the mission. The assignment was not to go to Shechem, it was to check on the welfare of the other boys. So when Joseph discovered his brothers weren't at Shechem, he journeyed on to Dothan. That added another fifteen miles to his journey by foot or by donkey. He could have returned to Hebron and told his father the boys weren't at Shechem. Instead, he knew what his father would have wanted him to do and he did it. He thought of reasons to complete his mission, not reasons to abandon it.

BROTHERS' RECEPTION

Joseph responded to Jacob's request and elicited an unforeseen response from his brothers.

The Brothers' Plot

Verse 18 tells us that when the brothers saw Joseph approaching, their resentment immediately rose to the surface. They considered killing Joseph and telling their father that a wild beast had devoured him. Nice brothers!

The thing that allowed them to identify him from afar—his long, flowing white robe—was the same thing that reminded them of why they hated him: He was Jacob's favorite son. The police today would call this a "premeditated" crime, not a crime of passion. Their simmering rage evolved into a murderous plot in the time between their spotting him and his arrival.

Reuben's Proposal

Instead of killing Joseph, Reuben urged his brothers to spare his life but throw him into a nearby cistern from which he would be unable to escape. Archaeologists have discovered cisterns in Palestine with skeletons in the bottom of them, so apparently this was not a novel tactic but a well-known way of dispensing with one's enemies.

Interestingly, the text of verse 22 ends with this note concerning Reuben's proposal: "that he might deliver [Joseph] out of their hands, and bring him back to his father." Apparently Reuben was not as ruthless as his brothers. His plan was to save Joseph's life— to help him escape so he could return home to Jacob. Though his plan didn't work out, we have to give him credit for having something resembling a conscience.

So they put Joseph into the cistern and "sat down to eat a meal" (verse 25). Amazing! These guys threw their brother into a cistern, apparently to die (except for Reuben), and then sat down a few feet away to have a sandwich! We know from Genesis 42:21 that Joseph was pleading with his brothers from the cistern while they sat there eating their lunch. I suppose we shouldn't be too surprised at their callousness given what Simeon and Levi did to the men of Shechem (Genesis 34).

Their actions are not uncommon in the human race. Often when people don't like the message, they shoot the messenger. And Joseph's brothers definitely did not like the message he had given them based on his dreams. The best way to get rid of the dreams is to get rid of the dreamer.

Judah's Plan

In verses 25–28 of chapter 37, we discover what actually happened to Joseph. The brothers saw a caravan of traders approaching, and Judah had an idea: "The boy's no good to us dead. Let's at least make a few dollars off him and sell him to the Ishmaelites." So the traders gave the brothers twenty shekels of silver and took Joseph with them to Egypt to sell as a slave.

Again, how hard must these brothers' hearts have been to have stood there negotiating a price with the traders in front of Joseph?

Reuben's Panic

Reuben must have been off tending to the sheep while this transaction took place. When he returned, he was horrified to discover what happened—that Joseph had been sold to the Ishmaelite traders (verses 29–30).

Reuben is an interesting character. He was the oldest brother and demonstrated a measure of influence and leadership, sparing Joseph's life. Reuben could have been bitter toward Joseph since he had been excluded from his inheritance as the firstborn of Leah and replaced by Joseph who was the firstborn of Jacob's other wife, Rachel (Genesis 35:22). But Reuben saved Joseph's life and panicked when he discovered the other boys had sent him off to Egypt with the traders. Reuben was no doubt fearful of Jacob's reaction since he would be held most accountable for Joseph's fate as the oldest of the brothers.

At the end of Jacob's life, it's obvious he didn't hold Reuben in very high regard. The "blessing" he gave his oldest son was an anti-blessing, if anything: "Unstable as water, you shall not excel, because you went up to your father's bed" (Genesis 49:4). Reuben sleeping with Jacob's concubine was bad enough, but allowing his father's favorite son to disappear would likely be worse. From Reuben's reaction years later in Egypt, it is obvious he worried about this event for years (Genesis 42:22).

When Reuben returned to their camp and discovered what his brothers had done, his primary concern was for himself: "The lad is no more; and I, where shall I go" (Genesis 37:30). Once we get involved in sin, we always focus on our own safety rather than the well-being of others. It is self-centeredness that motivates sin, and it is sin that motivates self-centeredness—a vicious cycle. How often do parents say, "Oh, what will people think of me?" when their children sin? Sin causes us to lose sight of the true concern.

THE FALSE REPORT

Well, the deed is done, and now the boys have to figure out what to tell Jacob upon their return. Their choices were the same two as man has always had: lie or tell the truth, and they chose the former.

Purposeful Deception

They purposefully planned to deceive their father by killing a young goat and dipping Joseph's tunic in it and telling Jacob he was killed by a wild animal. It is interesting that Jacob reaped from his own sons the very deception he had sown in his own life. He had used the hairy skin of a goat to deceive his father Isaac into thinking he was Esau (Genesis 27:16). People say what goes around comes around. And the Bible says we reap what we sow. And that was soon to come true in Jacob's life as he was deceived into thinking his favorite son was dead.

It is not only horrible how these men treated their own brother, but even more shameful that they allowed their father to suffer such mental and emotional anguish for no reason.

Jacob's Remorse

Genesis tells us that thirty years after the "death" of Joseph, Jacob was still mourning the loss of his son (42:36–38; 44:27–29). That proves that Joseph was indeed the apple of Jacob's eye. And it's true that he was reaping what he sowed. But it's still difficult not to have compassion for this old man who spent the last decades of his life grieving without cause. I'm sure he blamed himself for having sent Joseph on the errand to check on his brothers. I wonder how those sons faced their father in Egypt the day they discovered Joseph was alive. No doubt Jacob learned the truth about what happened and grieved even more about the sad state of his sons' hearts.

BELIEVER'S RESPONSE

There are at least four lessons to learn from this event in the life of Joseph.

The Power of Envy

In Acts 7:9, we read why Joseph's brothers sold him into slavery: "And the patriarchs, becoming envious, sold Joseph into Egypt." Oh, the power of envy! Envy moved Cain to kill Abel and made Saul chase David. It was envy that kept the older brother from rejoicing when the prodigal son returned home. And it was envy that caused the Jews to deliver up Jesus to Pilate.

When the green sickness of envy crept into the hearts of ten brothers, even Reuben, there was no limit to what they would do to remove the object of their envy. Anyone who is indulging themselves in the poison of envy should contemplate the damage it caused in the life of Jacob's sons. It caused ten men to commit crimes against their brother and sentence their father to unspeakable grief for most of his remaining years.

The Pretense of Morality

Joseph's brothers fell into the trap of believing that a lesser evil was justified if it was done instead of the greater evil. Instead of killing their brother outright, they sold him into slavery where they had to know the chances were good that he would die anyway. But they justified their actions by not committing the murder itself. Instead, they made it possible for him to die another way. The lesser of two evils is not, by default, a righteous act. Evil is evil regardless. By feigning morality—". . . let not our hand be upon him, for he is our brother and our flesh"—they condemned themselves as guilty of the vilest hypocrisy. If they truly regarded Joseph as their brother, they never would have been envious of him, the beginning of all their sins.

Even when reporting the "death" of Joseph to their father, they never came out and said, "He is dead." Instead, they showed Jacob the bloody, torn tunic and let him draw the conclusion. Again, they patted themselves on the back for not lying.

Don't be tempted to think highly of yourself for sinning less. Sin is sin regardless of the self-righteousness with which it is committed.

The Penalty of Sin

Romans 6:23 says, "For the wages of sin is death." There is a penalty for sin; someone is always hurt by sin. Joseph was separated from his family for over thirty years and caused to suffer in prison in Egypt. Jacob was hurt by the loss of his son for the same period of time. Even the brothers suffered the defilement of their consciences and the hardening of their hearts against further sin.

The one who commits sin always suffers the most. The wages of sin is death of one sort or another.

The Providence of God

It is important to remember that God rules over all. In spite of the heinous sins committed by Joseph's brothers against him and against Jacob, God worked above it all and through it all to accomplish His purposes (Genesis 50:20). And the same is true for your sin and mine. Don't mistake that for a license to sin. Instead, recognize it for what it is: God's grace is greater than all our sin.

This part of Joseph's story is one of the most revealing in the Bible of the depths of human sin and depravity. Let it be a word of warning to you to steer clear of envy, deception, and pretentious morality. Depend on God's grace to prevent sin, not to salvage the remains of sin.

1. Turn to Genesis 37:12-26 to learn how Joseph's brothers betrayed him.

   a. Where were Joseph's brothers watching over their flock? (verse 12)

   b. What did Jacob request of Joseph? (verse 14)

   c. Why do you think Jacob asked Joseph to carry out this task? What did Joseph's brothers do in the past that hindered their father's trust in them? (Genesis 34)

2. Joseph exhibited different character traits from his brothers that set him apart.

   a. What two aspects of obedience did he possess?

      1. _____ obedience

      2. _____ obedience

   b. Even though his brothers didn't like him, why do you think Joseph obeyed his father's request?

c. Did Joseph have the opportunity to abandon his mission? Where were his brothers actually located? (Genesis 37:17)

d. Have you faced similar circumstances in your life in which you wanted to give up but knew you had to obey? Explain.

3. Turn to the section titled "Brothers' Reception."

   a. When Joseph finally arrived at the place where his brothers were located, what did they conspire to do? (verses 18-20)

   b. When Reuben, the oldest brother, heard their plot, how did he respond? (verses 21-22)

   c. What might have motivated Reuben to respond that way?

   d. What did the brothers end up doing with Joseph? After doing so, how did they spend their time? (verses 24-25)

   e. When a caravan of traders approached, what did Judah suggest they do with Joseph? (verses 25-27)

f. When Reuben returned to the pit and realized his brother was gone, how did he react? (verses 29-30) For whom was he most concerned?

g. Why do you think Reuben responded that way? For what reason was he more fearful than his brothers that Joseph was gone?

4. Joseph's brothers planned on deceiving their father once they returned to Canaan.

a. What piece of clothing did they strip Joseph of, and what did they tell Jacob? (verses 31-32)

b. In what way does this situation in Jacob's life relate to the situation he encountered in the past with his own brother? (Genesis 27:16)

c. Do you think Jacob was reaping what he sowed? Why do you think God allowed him to face such a difficult trial?

d. How long after Joseph "died" did Jacob still mourn? ("Jacob's Remorse")

5. Read Acts 7:9.

   a. What attribute did Joseph's brothers possess, initially leading them to sell him into Egypt?

   b. How do you think his brothers justified throwing Joseph into the pit? Does that make their sin any better?

   c. What is often the result when people try to cover their sins? Who does sin most affect—the one against whom the sin was committed or the one who committed the sin?

DID YOU KNOW?

Time moved slowly in the Old Testament. The geographical range of this story was from Hebron in the south of Canaan to Dothan in the north. Joseph's brothers moved the herds from Hebron to Shechem, a distance of about forty-five miles. Moving the herds at one mile per hour, that trip would have taken most of a week. Another fifteen miles to Dothan was another two or three days. The same for the return trip to Hebron. When Joseph went to check on the brothers, he might have traveled a bit faster; but it was still a good four or five days to find his brothers at Dothan. Given travel time, and the weeks the brothers spent grazing the herds, Jacob was likely out of touch with his sons for several months.

THE WORST CHAPTER IN THE BIBLE

Genesis 38:1–30

In this lesson we discover the reason for the perfect placement of a seemingly misplaced chapter in Genesis.

OUTLINE

The story of Joseph begins well in Genesis 37. Then it seems the story disappears in Genesis 38. Believing that with God there is always a reason, careful study reveals why Genesis 38, though not about Joseph, is critical to the story of providence of which Joseph is the main character.

I. The Providence of God
   A. The Sin of Judah
   B. The Shame of Judah
   C. The Sons of Judah

II. The Purpose of the Chapter
   A. The Concern of God for His People
   B. The Contrast Between the Spirit and the Flesh
   C. The Corruption of Sin in a Family
   D. The Continuing Story of God's Grace

D id the title of this lesson catch your attention? The events described in Genesis 38 leave a black mark on the memory of anyone who reads this chapter. And they raise two questions right from the start. First, why is this chapter here in such plain language, much of which offends our sensibilities? And second, why would God interrupt the story of Joseph right after it began in chapter 37 to tell a story that has nothing to do with him? We will waste no time in getting into this unusual story to answer those questions.

THE PROVIDENCE OF GOD

The story of Joseph, from beginning to end, is a story of the providence of God—how He is always at work behind the scenes in this life to accomplish His purposes. We have seen His providence at work in moving Joseph to Egypt and in the occasion of the famine in Canaan that took Jacob's family to Egypt. And in Genesis 38, we will see how moral darkness is in the control of God's providence as well. We will see the family of Jacob in danger of succumbing to grave immorality in Canaan and how it was necessary for them to be removed from that danger until a later time.

There are three sections to our study of God's providence: Judah's sin (verses 1–11), Judah's shame (verses 12–23), and Judah's sons (verses 24–30). After studying the details of these events, we will reflect on the purpose of including this story at this point in Genesis.

The Sin of Judah

Judah was the son of Jacob who came up with the idea of selling Joseph to the Ishmaelite traders on their way to Egypt (Genesis 37:26). The brothers returned to Hebron, to their father Jacob, with the bad news of Joseph's "demise." Shortly after those events, we are told (verse 1) that Judah married a Canaanite woman in a town not far from Hebron, who bore him three sons: Er, Onan, and Shelah.

Judah was like the prodigal son in the story told by Jesus, the one who was completely out of God's and his father's will when he left home. Judah apparently had little or no spiritual light in his heart. He sold his brother for twenty pieces of silver and now unites himself to a pagan woman and has children with her. He seems to have had no connection to his father's God, the God of Abraham, Isaac, and Jacob.

Years passed and the firstborn of Judah's sons, Er, grew up and married a woman named Tamar (verse 6). For unnamed reasons, Er "was wicked in the sight of the Lord, and the Lord killed him" (verse 7). Tamar was now a widow, so Judah told his second son, Onan, to have relations with Tamar so there would be an heir to carry on the line of Er. This was common practice in the culture of the day and would become formalized in the Mosaic Law when passing on a family's parcel of property in the promised land became an important matter.

Onan went in to Tamar but had no intention of fathering a son that would not be his, so he spilled his seed on the ground so Tamar would not become pregnant (verse 9). This act angered the Lord, and Onan's life was taken as well. So Judah had now lost two sons and still had a widowed daughter-in-law. Judah did not send his youngest son, Shelah, in to Tamar. Perhaps he was too young, or perhaps Judah feared losing him as well (verse 11). So Judah promised Tamar that when Shelah was older, he would go in to her and provide a child to perpetuate his brother's name and provide an heir. So he sent Tamar home to her father's house to live.

All of this happened because Judah went somewhere and did something he never should have done. Two young men were dead and a widow was back home in her parents' house.

The Shame of Judah

The story gets darker as Judah compounded his sins by going in to what he thought was a harlot but was actually his daughter-in-law, Tamar.

In time, Judah's own wife died and he was now without a wife to provide him relational comfort. When Judah went with one of his Canaanite friends to visit his sheepshearers in Timnah, Tamar learned of his intentions and saw an opportunity to provide an heir for herself through her former husband's family. We also learn that Shelah, Judah's third son, was now grown but had not been given to Tamar as promised to provide her with an heir (verse 14). So Tamar decided to take matters into her own hands.

It was the custom that if a widow's former husband had no brothers who could provide her with an heir, then her former father-in-law (or the nearest male relative) could also provide the same service. Knowing that Judah would not likely be willing to do that after several years had passed, she conceived a plan to trick him into impregnating her.

Tamar dressed and positioned herself in such a way that when Judah passed by on his way to Timnah, he would think she was a harlot. (She "covered herself with a veil" [verse 14] so Judah wouldn't recognize her.) And her plan worked perfectly. When Judah passed by, he negotiated a price with what he thought was a harlot by the road. He promised to send her a young goat from his flock, but she demanded a pledge—collateral, if you will—that she would hold until the goat was delivered. She demanded Judah's "signet and cord, and [his] staff," to which he agreed (verse 18). So Judah went in and had relations with Tamar and she became pregnant by him.

The annual shearing of the sheep in that day was a celebratory event. The wool would be gathered and sold or kept to be woven— it was a time of profit and partying for those who had flocks they had been shepherding all year. Judah was looking forward to being cheered up after the death of his wife and, in that spirit, availed himself of the "harlot" he encountered. Tamar saw it as the perfect opportunity to have her husband's bloodline reestablished through his father, Judah. So lying (Judah's, by not giving Tamar his son Shelah) and deceit (Tamar's, by pretending to be a harlot to entrap Judah) find their way once again into Jacob's household. The seeds he sowed earlier in his life continue to bear fruit.

Judah's signet was likely a cylinder seal carried on a cord around the neck, engraved with identifying marks. It would serve like the modern stamp of a notary. When clay documents were pre- pared for business purposes, a cylinder seal would be rolled across the damp clay, leaving the owner's identifying mark. All of these items—signet, cord, and staff—said "Judah" to anyone who would look at them. The deal was that he would leave those items in Tamar's possession until he delivered the goat in payment for her services, at which time she would give back his property.

Unfortunately for Judah, the story now gets darker. He sent the goat in payment by a friend; but the friend returned, saying he couldn't find the harlot. Judah knew if he started asking around, trying to find her, it might be discovered that he was the one who went in to her, which he didn't want. So he decided to let her keep the signet, cord, and staff and that would be the end of it.

In verse 24, we learn that three months later, it was told to Judah that Tamar was pregnant and that it must be by means of immorality on her part. Judah was outraged that his daughter-in- law had done such a thing and demanded that she be burned. But Tamar produced the signet, cord, and staff and said, "By the man to whom these belong, I am with child" (verse 25). Uh-oh. Judah had been found out. It was obvious to all concerned that Judah was the one who had gotten Tamar pregnant.

As often happens with the self-righteous, the revelation of their own sins becomes immediate motivation for repentance and sorrow. When it became apparent that he was the father of Tamar's child, he suddenly stopped his talk of burning his former daughter-in-law. In fact, he said, "She has been more righteous than I, because I did not give her to Shelah my son" (verse 26).

The Sons of Judah

When it was time for Tamar to deliver, it was discovered she was carrying twins. When the first child stuck its hand out, the midwife put a scarlet thread around its wrist to signify him as the firstborn. But then he pulled his hand back in and his twin brother came out, followed by the twin with the scarlet thread on his wrist. The one who came out first was named Perez ("breaking out") and the one with the scarlet thread was named Zerah (possibly "scarlet"). It will be important that you remember "Perez" as we turn to consider God's purposes for the inclusion of this chapter.

THE PURPOSE OF THE CHAPTER

There are four ways we can profit from what some have called a worthless chapter in God's Word.

The Concern of God for His People

First, picture what is called on high-tech televisions, picture-in-picture. While this debauched story is taking place in Canaan, in a second window, happening at the same time, we can see Joseph being sold to Potiphar in Egypt. The two events are connected by the phrase "at that time" in Genesis 38:1, which picks up 37:36 describing Joseph being sold as a slave in Egypt.

While Jacob's sons were in Canaan intermarrying with Canaanite women, at the same time Joseph was going ahead of them to prepare a place of sanctuary for them in Egypt. This wasn't a plan in any human mind, but it was definitely a plan in the mind of God. So chapter 37—Joseph's sale into slavery in Egypt—is connected to chapter 38 by the little phrase "at that time." It shows God's continuing concern for His people, the descendants of Abraham. While they were coming unraveled in Canaan like a loose thread on a hem, God was preparing a place for them to be put back together in Egypt where they would be free from the evil they weren't spiritually strong enough to resist.

In Egypt the family of Jacob grew for 430 years, isolated and shunned by the Egyptians (Genesis 43:32; 46:34), protected from intermarrying with pagans and losing their identity.

The Contrast Between the Spirit and the Flesh

If we were to read ahead to Genesis 39, we would see Joseph facing sexual temptation in the house of Potiphar as "Mrs." Potiphar attempted to seduce him. But we also read in Genesis 41 that Joseph was a man filled with the Spirit of God (verse 38). So unlike Judah, Joseph—who had the same upbringing as his older brother—yielded to the Spirit and not to the flesh. He resisted Mrs. Potiphar's temptation and fled the scene, refusing to dishonor his earthly and heavenly masters. Joseph maintained his integrity while Judah created a huge black mark on his father's family's name.

As we find so often in Scripture (Abraham vs. Lot, Mary vs. Judas), contrasts help us see the real picture better. And the contrast between Judah (the flesh) and Joseph (the Spirit) could not be more clear. Joseph shows us that it is possible to live in a world of sin and remain faithful and true.

The Corruption of Sin in a Family

In this story we are shown the failure of yet another of Jacob's sons. First, there were Simeon and Levi who killed the men of Shechem, then Reuben who slept with his father's concubine, and now Judah who married a pagan and then impregnated his own daughter-in-law.

I appreciate the teaching I have heard that stresses the critical role of the father as the spiritual "umbrella" in the family. As a man's wife and children gather beneath his umbrella of righteousness, they are shielded from the temptation and ungodliness falling around them. I believe the more faithful a man is in walking in righteousness, the greater the likelihood that his wife and children will walk in righteousness as well.

It's easy to see how Jacob reaped the results of his own sin. During the earlier years of his life, during his children's formative years, Jacob was not an umbrella of spiritual protection for them—and the results became evident when they became men. Every father should take to heart the impact of Jacob's sins on his own sons.

The Continuing Story of God's Grace

This is a chapter in the Bible of extremes. It shows the extreme depravity of man, but it also shows the extreme grace of God. We have seen in previous lessons how God never gave up on Jacob until he finally surrendered. All across the Middle East, God followed Jacob, even blessing him in spite of Jacob's always returning to his old ways of deceit and manipulation. And we find God's grace continuing to work through Jacob's descendants, redeeming something for His own glory out of the mistakes they made.

As tawdry as the tale of Judah and Tamar is, we learn later in the Bible that God allowed the blood of Judah and Tamar to flow through Messiah's veins. We can see this by looking at a couple of key Scripture passages.

Genesis 49:8–12 records Jacob's blessing of Judah in which he referred to the coming of "Shiloh," a reference to the Messiah. This prophetic word was given in Egypt, long after Judah's relationship with Tamar. So in spite of his sins, God's grace is still at work in Judah's life as the line through which Messiah would come.

Ruth 4:18–22 reveals that one of the twins of Judah and Tamar, the one named Perez, became the ancestor of king David—again, another link in the Messianic chain (repeated in Matthew 1:3–5). Only God's always-at-work grace could take the product of a union like Judah and Tamar's and use it for His glory. Perez stands as a testament for all who think their standing in this life disqualifies them to be used by God.

I don't know where you are in your life. Perhaps you have made some seriously bad choices like Judah, or perhaps you are suffering the effects of others' choices like Perez. But whoever and wherever you are, you are not beyond the extent of God's grace. At the same time Judah was making choices that could have led to calamity for Jacob's family, God was preparing a safe haven for them in Egypt through Joseph.

That's the reason God put Genesis 38 in the Bible—to show you that with God, all is never lost.

APPLICATION

1. Turn to Genesis 38:1-30 to catch a glimpse of the life of Joseph's brother Judah.

   a. When Judah left his family, whom did he marry? Why was this considered a sin? (verses 1-2)

   b. What story did Jesus tell that relates closely to the story of Judah? Did Judah seem to have any connection to his father's God?

   c. How many sons did Judah and his wife have? List them in order from youngest to oldest. (verses 3-5)

   d. Who was to be wed to Judah's firstborn son? But because of his wickedness, what did the Lord do to him? (verses 6-7)

   e. What became of the second son, and why did he refuse to comply? (verses 8-9) How did the Lord respond to his actions? (verse 10)

   f. What did Judah promise Tamar in regard to his youngest son? Where did he send her? (verse 11)

2. Eventually, Judah's own wife died and he was left alone.

   a. When Tamar found out that her father-in-law was to travel to Timnah, what did she do? (verses 12-14)

   b. What did Judah assume of Tamar? (verse 15) Did Tamar's plan work out just as she hoped? (verses 16-18)

   c. Why do you think Tamar deceived Judah into impregnating her?

   d. Have you ever been deceived in a way that changed your entire life? What became of that situation?

   e. When Judah eventually found out that Tamar was the harlot and was pregnant, how did he react? (verse 24) What did he remember as he came to his senses? (verse 26)

3. Turn to the section titled "The Purpose of the Chapter."

   a. While Jacob's son committed this sin, where was Joseph?

   b. What was God preparing for Jacob's family in Egypt?

c. What was different about Joseph when compared to his brothers? (Genesis 41:38)

d. Looking at Joseph's life, what can we learn about living in an environment of sin?

4. How might Jacob's earlier actions have influenced the actions of his own children?

a. Despite their actions, did God ever turn His back on Jacob?

b. What character trait of God's should we also exhibit when we've been wronged? What lesson can we learn from Genesis 38 that exemplifies this?

DID YOU KNOW?

The idea of the brother of a deceased husband fathering children for his sister-in-law was a custom in the ancient world before it was formalized in the Mosaic Law. Moses codified the obligation of levirate (from Latin *levir*, "brother-in-law") marriage in Deuteronomy 25:5–6. The purpose was for the dead husband's firstborn son to take the name of his father so that the father's "name may not be blotted out in Israel" (verse 6). In Ruth we find the idea of levirate marriage extended to the nearest living relative of Ruth (Ruth 2:20; 4:1–6). That relative gave up the right to Boaz who married Ruth.

THE TEST OF PURITY

Genesis 39:1–12

*In this lesson we learn how Joseph passed
the tests of prosperity and purity.*

OUTLINE

Joseph might be considered a wimp today since he turned down
two opportunities that many men would embrace: the chance to
use prosperity for personal gain and to sacrifice purity for personal
satisfaction. In spite of those temptations, Joseph remained true to
himself and his God.

I. The Test of Prosperity
  A. Prominence
  B. Position
  C. Power
  D. Popularity
  E. Physique

II. The Test of Purity
  A. The Power of Temptation
  B. The Power Over Temptation

W hen we left Joseph at the end of chapter 37, he was on his way to Egypt, the property of Ishmaelite traders. We looked at the story of Judah in chapter 38 in the last lesson, and we pick up the story of Joseph again in Genesis 39.

When we meet Joseph in Egypt, he has probably been there about ten years and is around twenty-seven years old. Put on the slave trade block along with other captives, he likely stood out by virtue of being a Hebrew and (as we will soon learn) his handsome appearance. He was purchased by a man named Potiphar, the captain of the pharaoh's bodyguard (verse 1). In time, Joseph was made the chief steward of Potiphar's household. So Joseph has gone from being the favorite son of his father to a slave of the captain of the secret police in Egypt.

I have found it interesting to note that of all the patriarchs, Joseph never had a face-to-face meeting with God. Abraham, Isaac, and Jacob did, but Joseph did not. Yet Joseph's life has more detail about the providential oversight of God than his forefathers' lives combined. It's a good reminder that we don't have to have the most dramatic relationship with God in terms of "hearing from God" to know that He is intimately involved in the affairs of our lives.

In this lesson we'll look at two tests Joseph faced—and passed with God's help: the test of prosperity and the test of purity.

THE TEST OF PROSPERITY

It would be hard to find a greater progression through the ranks of prosperity than that of Joseph in Potiphar's household. The first six verses of chapter 39 mention "prosperity," "success," "favor," and "blessed" several times with regard to Joseph.

Prominence

First, Joseph achieved a prominent position. He went from being a slave on the bottom rung of importance to being made the over-seer of all of Potiphar's household. He was, in a sense, the "chief of staff" of Potiphar's house. By virtue of Potiphar's rank in Pharaoh's court, his holdings would have been large, which meant Joseph's job as overseer was a weighty one. All the most important officers in Egypt would have come to know who Joseph was, and he would have met many of them personally. Potiphar no doubt spoke highly of Joseph, the young Hebrew from Canaan, when talking with his associates in Pharaoh's court.

Position

In several ways, we are told about Joseph's position in Potiphar's household. He was "overseer of [Potiphar's] house" (verse 4), overseer of "all that [Potiphar] had" (verse 5), to such an extent that Potiphar "did not know what he had except for the bread which he ate" (verse 6). And Joseph himself says, when defending himself against Potiphar's wife's advances, that there was no one greater in Potiphar's house than he (Joseph)—that Potiphar had turned over everything he had to Joseph (verses 8–9).

In other words, Joseph was in complete control of Potiphar's house. Every businessman knows it is a dangerous thing to turn over the "keys to the kingdom" to a subordinate unless you are absolutely confident that person is trustworthy. And that is what Joseph was to Potiphar: someone who could be trusted.

Power

Along with prominence and position came power, of course. The more responsible Joseph became, the more power he gained. Joseph was given both responsibility and authority—the two things every leader needs to succeed. The question was whether Joseph would use his power to serve his master or subvert his master's plans. Because Joseph was a godly man, he used his power to serve Potiphar in all he did.

Popularity

I imagine Joseph was like a breath of fresh air in the house of Potiphar. God blessed everything Joseph touched, and that meant that Potiphar's house was blessed as well. Verse 5 tells us that "the Lord blessed the Egyptian's house for Joseph's sake; and the blessing of the Lord was on all that he had in the house and in the field." That means everything Potiphar had—his businesses, investments, relationships, his stature in the court—was multiplying in value. And it was all because of the blessing of God on Joseph. Joseph's popularity increased daily in the eyes of Potiphar and the rest of his servants. Things had never been better since Joseph arrived.

Physique

Verse 6 says, "Now Joseph was handsome in form and appearance." Perhaps Joseph inherited some of his mother's attractive appearance since she (Rachel) "was beautiful of form and appearance" (Genesis 29:17). The same words are used to describe the mother and the son. So we can settle the question forever of where children get their good looks—it's from their mothers!

It's interesting how little emphasis there is in the Bible on physical attractiveness. Joseph is only one of a handful of people I can find who are said to be attractive. Joseph was certainly one of them, but his attractiveness was about to become a thorn in his side.

THE TEST OF PURITY

Joseph passed the test of prosperity with flying colors, but it was now time for his purity to be tested. It is common for tests of various sorts to come when we are at the height of our success—think of David's test of purity with Bathsheba when he was at the height of his success as king of Israel. Somehow prosperity makes people think they can handle life on their own, forgetting it was God who made them prosperous to begin with.

"After these things" (verse 7—after Joseph's rise in power and popularity) "Mrs." Potiphar tried to entrap Joseph in a sexually immoral way. But Joseph refused, remaining loyal both to his master and to God. But it was a genuine test of his purity.

The Power of Temptation

Ancient cultures were very lascivious, full of sexual temptation. This was no small temptation Joseph was facing—it was as severe as anything in our modern culture and would not have been considered unusual at all in Joseph's day. I say that to point out that it is possible in our day and time to stand firm against temptation. Joseph did it in his day, and we can do it in ours. There were five aspects of Joseph's temptation that point out exactly how real a temptation it was—and how much Joseph was to be commended for resisting it.

1. A Surprise Temptation

    Joseph's temptation came like many do—as a surprise. Things were going so well in Potiphar's household; Joseph had done nothing to deserve what Mrs. Potiphar was trying to do to him. When we are prospering, we are often relaxed, living with our guard down. Joseph's temptation is a good argument for living on guard.

2. A Sustained Temptation

    When the temptation started, it was a surprise. When it continued, it was a matter of grave concern. Verse 10 says Mrs. Potiphar spoke to Joseph "day by day," trying to wear down his defenses. Anyone who has been tempted over time knows how resistance can be weakened.

3. A Secret Temptation

   This was a sin that, if Joseph committed, no one would ever know about. Either Potiphar's wife or Joseph could have banished the rest of the servants from the house and done whatever they wanted to. The truest test of a person's character is what they would do if they knew, with absolute certainty, that no one would ever find out. I imagine that a large part of our righteous behavior is less out of a desire to obey God than it is a fear of getting caught. But Joseph knew he probably wouldn't get caught and obeyed God anyway.

4. A Sensible Temptation

   Almost all temptations have a measure of rationality about them—it's how we justify giving in to them. In Joseph's case, he could have reasoned that it would have been to his advantage to give in to Mrs. Potiphar's desires; that it would have given him an inside track to even greater influence. He could also have reasoned that not to give in to her would have been dangerous (which it turned out to be). Joseph could easily have rationalized this sin. But he chose to honor God and not be "reasonable" about it.

5. A Subtle Temptation

   Finally, there are always aspects of temptation beneath the surface. Yes, Joseph was being tempted sexually. But he was also a man who had been rejected by his own brothers. It would have been easy to succumb to the need to be wanted and affirmed. Many men who give in to sexual temptation do so for non-sexual reasons. And Joseph could have done that as well. But he chose to stand alone in spite of his need for emotional companionship and intimacy.

These five aspects of Joseph's temptation combined to make this a serious test of his commitment to purity. It's easy to read this story in a few verses of Scripture and forget that this played out over a lengthy period, that Joseph spent hours and hours agonizing over this situation, trying to maintain his strength. He was a man like any other, dealing with the reality of temptation.

We've seen the power *of* the temptation and now we'll look at the power *over* temptation.

The Power Over Temptation

I can see at least five things that were true of Joseph that helped him overcome the temptation to sin. And they can help us if we will adopt them.

1. Joseph had convictions before crisis.

Verses 7–8 seem to describe the first time Potiphar's wife approached Joseph with her invitation to immorality. His response? He immediately refused. In other words, his instinctive reaction was to say NO! Why was No his instinctive reaction instead of Yes? Because he had been walking with God and had rehearsed this answer in his mind many times before. The first key to overcoming temptation is to know what the answer is before the temptation presents itself.

I have preached to young people many times that the back seat of a car is no place to decide what your response to temptation is going to be. And the same is true for adults as well. If we don't know what we believe about money, sex, telling the truth, keeping our word, and all the other issues of life which, in the world, can go either way, then we are likely to go the way of the world. Joseph had said No to himself many times before ever saying it to Potiphar's wife.

2. Joseph knew love involved loyalty.

Joseph placed a high value on loyalty. In verses 8–9, he tells Potiphar's wife that he would never dishonor the trust that Potiphar had placed in him. Nor would he dishonor God. Joseph knew that every sin against man was ultimately a sin against God. He connected the wickedness he was being asked to commit against Potiphar as a sin against God (verse 9).

Somehow modern Americans, indeed many Christians, especially young people, have adopted the idea that sexual activity is a matter of privacy between consenting adults; that it's no one's business but theirs. Leaving God out of it for the moment, we know that's not true. Sin always reverberates and impacts people who were not involved in it. Joseph knew that he was not an isolated moral agent, that there would be human and divine ramifications for everything he chose to do. And he decided to remain loyal to three people: himself, his master, and his God.

3. Joseph had sense to avoid the source.

Genesis doesn't tell us anything about Mrs. Potiphar, nor do any secular sources. But I imagine that she was beautiful given her husband's prominence and opportunity to pick who he wanted for a wife. And she also appears to be persistent and clever—verse 10 tells us that she "spoke to Joseph day by day." We've already noted the time factor here, but don't miss the "spoke to" part. I imagine she backed off from her original bold proposal that Joseph refused and began trying other methods, trying to wear down his resistance.

But what did Joseph do? Not only did he refuse to sleep with her, he refused "to be with her" (verse 10). He wouldn't even go near her in order not to listen to her words. Joseph was avoiding the source of the temptation. He didn't try to prove how strong he was by hanging out with Potiphar's wife. He avoided her altogether. I have talked with men who admit to being sexually tempted by a woman in their office who don't see the need to change jobs! You can't get close to fire without being burned—so Joseph avoided the flame.

4. Joseph was still shocked by sin.

Joseph was still an innocent in many ways, certainly compared to his brothers and the culture of Egypt. He still had a sense of purity and godliness about him that caused him to be shocked by the idea of sin.

I believe that is missing in the Christian community today. There is very little that shocks us when it comes to what we see on television, read in magazines, or see in movies. We have concluded that sin is normal and nothing to be offended by or angry at. I can remember as a child when our family got its first television with a snowy, small, round screen. I think my father thought he had capitulated to the dark side when he bought it, and he monitored what we watched very carefully. He probably turned off more beer commercials than anyone in the history of television.

But who does that today? Not many people. We are no longer shocked by sin and indecency. Joseph was shocked when Mrs. Potiphar proposed to him: "How then can I do this great wickedness, and sin against God?" (verse 9).

5. Joseph knew retreat was better than defeat.

When Mrs. Potiphar couldn't get Joseph to agree willingly, she tried to force the issue. She grabbed hold of his robe and tried to force him to comply with her desires. But Joseph slipped out of his robe and fled from the house, leaving her holding what he had been wearing. Joseph knew he was better off without his coat than without his character.

Sometimes the only way to defeat temptation is to run from it—fast! Sexual sin is the only situation in which we are told to run from the sin (2 Timothy 2:22). In other cases we're told to resist the devil and he will run. But there's something about the power of physical desire that puts it in a different category. Retreat is better than defeat when it comes to any sin, but especially to one that can get out of control as quickly as the one Joseph faced.

I hope you will take Joseph's experience to heart. Recognize the power *of* temptation and the principles for gaining victory *over* temptation.

1. Turn to Genesis 39:1-12—the test of Joseph's prosperity and purity.

   a. How was God's blessing being fulfilled in verse 3?

   b. With whom did Joseph find favor in Egypt? What position of power did he acquire? (verse 4; see verse 1)

   c. What was his master merely knowledgeable of? (verse 6) Why do you think he trusted Joseph with all of his property?

2. Because the Lord blessed everything that Joseph touched, including his master's house, how might people have responded to his presence? (See verse 5.)

   a. In addition to the blessings Joseph received, what trait made him even more approachable? (verse 6)

   b. From whom did Joseph receive that trait? (Genesis 29:17)

3. Read Genesis 39:7-10 to learn about Joseph's temptation.

   a. What temptation did Joseph encounter? Who did the tempting? (verse 7)

   b. How did Joseph react? What was his immediate response? (verse 8)

   c. What was Joseph more concerned about—getting caught by Potiphar or disobeying God? (verse 9)

   d. In order to avoid temptation altogether, what did Joseph choose to do (or not to do)? (verse 10)

   e. As Joseph fled, what did he leave behind? (verses 11-12) How might this affect him in the future?

f. When in your own life have you resisted temptation? For what reason did you resist?

4. To what degree have you become desensitized to sin in our culture?

a. What is the only sin we are told to run from? (2 Timothy 2:22) Why do you think this sin is in a category all on its own? (1 Corinthians 6:18)

b. Just as Joseph put on a robe that allowed him to escape temptation and flee, what should we be clothed in that will allow us to do the same thing? (See Romans 13:14.)

c. What else should we clothe ourselves in? (See Ephesians 4:24 and Colossians 3:10.)

d. To what sins have you already said No in your heart? For what sins have you left the door of possibility open?

e. How can you get into the habit of saying No to temptation? Name a few ways in which this goal can be accomplished.

DID YOU KNOW?

Just as New Testament believers focus on God's unconditional love (*agape*), so Old Testament saints depended on God's loyalty (*hesed*). In the Old Testament, *hesed* is often translated as mercy (not giving what is deserved) or kindness (giving what isn't deserved) that are reflections of God's loyalty to His people. In the Psalms, it is often translated as lovingkindness, or loyal love. *Hesed*, loyal love, is at the heart of the covenants God made with His people. Along with *agape*, it is God's loyalty toward us that inspires us to show loyalty and love to Him—as Joseph did when he refused to dishonor God by sinning.

JOSEPH AND THE NEW MORALITY

Genesis 39:13–23

In this lesson we see Joseph maintaining his convictions in spite of his circumstances.

OUTLINE

There are modern theories of ethics that say, "If your goals are good, no one is hurt; and if your motivation is love, then you are free to do whatever you want." Joseph didn't let his situation determine his ethics. He maintained his beliefs regardless of how circumstances changed.

I. **Prosperity Is Not a Matter of Circumstances but a Matter of Character**

II. **Perspective Comes From Seeing God in Every Circumstance**

III. **Present Problems Often Prepare Us for Future Positions**

IV. **Righteousness Is Not Always Immediately Rewarded**

In the previous lesson, we covered the heart of Joseph's strong stand against temptation. We looked at the power *of* temptation and Joseph's power *over* temptation. As solid as Joseph's actions appear to us from a biblical perspective, there are some who would argue that Joseph acted a little too hastily, that it might have been acceptable for him to enter into a relationship with Mrs. Potiphar, that he perhaps was too hard on himself by denying the pleasure that presented itself to him.

There is a new morality, a modern reinterpretation of what is right and what is wrong, that has made itself known in today's world. This new morality surfaced back in the 1960s under the label "situational ethics." This philosophy said that sin depends on the situation—that there is no always-right and always-wrong answer.

In 1963 an Anglican bishop named John A. T. Robinson wrote a book titled *Honest to God*. In that book was a chapter titled "The New Morality." Robinson's views on situational ethics, or the new morality, gained a wide hearing when he delivered a series of lectures on the subject at Liverpool Cathedral in England. His argument was that the "old morality" (what Joseph practiced— a belief in a firm right and wrong) was a perversion of the New Testament since it advocated slavery to a legalistic code of law rather than adherence to Christ's law of love.

In 1966, Robinson's views gained a boost when an American Episcopal priest named Joseph Fletcher, who became Professor of Social Ethics at the Episcopal Theological School of Cambridge, Massachusetts, began expanding on Robinson's views. Fletcher wrote *Situation Ethics—The New Morality and Moral Responsibility* in 1966 in which he announced a new day of freedom from the legalism of the Bible's strict codes of conduct. Robinson and Fletcher taught that love trumped law, that when a person did the most loving thing in any given situation, he was doing the right thing. It was a form of permissiveness that said, "If no one gets hurt then anything goes." It was a humanistic philosophy based on the belief that man is basically good and that given the right environment, he will always make right and loving choices.

One has to wonder if these two men, and those who followed them in this nonbiblical belief, had been living in the real world. There is no shortage of evidence, wherever one looks in the world, that even in the best of circumstances, men don't always do the right thing or the most loving thing. The most educated, advantaged, and prosperous of human beings choose to do hurtful things time after time.

According to the new morality, all laws, codes, and rules are outmoded and obsolete—except for the law of love as determined by the situation one is in. Love is determined by the situation one is in and the greatest good—if doing something "wrong" results in a greater good taking place, then the wrong thing becomes right.

In the last lesson, we saw that Joseph did not allow the situation he was in to determine his morality. He had convictions before the crisis came about. He interpreted the situation in light of his morals instead of letting the situation dictate his morals. Joseph was obviously operating under the "old" morality.

In one of his books, Joseph Fletcher gives an illustration of how one goes about making a moral decision in a difficult situation. He takes the plot of a story written by N. Richard Nash about a rainmaker who makes his living convincing farmers and ranchers that he can make it rain. At a particular ranch, the rainmaker meets the rancher's daughter who, while attractive, was rather shy and homely. He decides he can boost this young woman's sense of self-image and self-confidence by making love to her, which he does. When the girl's brother finds out, he is ready to kill the rainmaker until their father enters the scene. He grabs the gun from his son and says, "Noah, you're so full of what's right, you can't see what's good."

There you have situational ethics in a nutshell: committing fornication in order to help a young woman feel better about herself. In other words, the end justifies the means. Because the rainmaker had a noble goal in mind—the elevation of the young woman's sense of self-worth—his actions were loving and good. Fletcher would say that no one was hurt in the process, and that the brother's actions were only because of his living in the world of the old morality. It was the brother's outmoded beliefs that were wrong, not the rainmaker's actions.

Joseph, according to Fletcher, should have come out alright in his dealing with Potiphar's wife. His intentions were good, no one was hurt, but Joseph ended up in prison. We pick up the story of Joseph's old morality in Genesis 39.

Joseph refused, over the course of many days, to give in to Mrs. Potiphar's seductions. She finally grabbed at him and Joseph only escaped by wriggling out of his robe and fleeing. She then used his garment to frame Joseph, saying he had attacked her in the house: ". . . so it happened, as I lifted my voice and cried out, that he left his garment with me and fled outside" (verse 18). She then tried to blame Joseph's alleged attack on her husband, Potiphar, saying it was his fault by bringing the Hebrew slave into their home. Potiphar had Joseph thrown into prison.

Joseph did right, but everything turned out wrong—for the second time. The first time was when he obeyed his father and went to search for his brothers in Shechem and got sold into slavery. And now this. He maintained his integrity and would not commit sexual sin with his master's wife, and he ended up in prison.

If ethics are based only on our good intentions, then clearly Joseph's ethics don't work. Twice he did the right things, and twice he suffered. According to situational ethics, Joseph would have expected to be rewarded for doing the right thing. Instead, he was caused to suffer both times.

The old morality—the biblical morality—has the answer: We don't do right or wrong because of what we think we'll get out of it. We do right, and don't do wrong, because it is the will of God. Our motivation is simple: God is the judge who establishes right and wrong, and we do everything out of obedience to Him.

Now, there is a tension in this belief because it is true that God promises to bless our obedience. So we give to God and obey God not to get from God but because it is what pleases Him. It is true that we will reap what we sow; and if we sow to the will of God, we will reap according to the will of God. But that is secondary to the matter of obedience. And that is why Joseph did what he did. And that is also why he was not upset with the results. We have no record in Scripture of Joseph being angry with God after being sold into slavery or thrown into prison.

It is interesting that Joseph actually got off quite easily since the punishment for what he was accused of was usually torture and death. Don't forget that Potiphar was head of the pharaoh's bodyguard, or secret police. He could execute anyone he wanted to. But he didn't execute Joseph. What's going on here? Note that in verse 19 it says that Potiphar's "anger was aroused," but it doesn't say at whom. I believe Potiphar was angry at his wife, not Joseph. I think he knew his wife better than we realize at the first reading of this story. Potiphar had to put Joseph in prison because he would have left himself open to blame if he hadn't. I think Potiphar knew Joseph well enough to know that he couldn't have done what

Mrs. Potiphar accused him of. And I think Potiphar knew his wife well enough to know she was capable of falsely accusing Joseph.

And Potiphar was right about Joseph—the cream continued to rise to the top even in prison. He was a leader in his home, a leader in Potiphar's home, and he became a leader in prison. He was put in charge of all the other prisoners, receiving full authority from the prison master to run things as he saw fit (verses 22–23). Joseph seems to have been a leader, a man blessed by God to spread God's influence wherever he went and whatever he did. Potiphar's suspicions about Joseph's innocence were probably confirmed as he watched how he acted in prison. He had to keep Joseph confined long enough (two years—Genesis 41:1) for the uproar over him to die down.

Life wasn't a bed of roses for Joseph in prison. In Psalm 105:18 (Psalm 105 devotes several verses to a summary of Joseph's life) we learn that, "They hurt his feet with fetters, he was laid in irons." Potiphar let Joseph be treated like a regular prisoner until he was released and made the supervisor of the whole operation.

There are four important applications to grasp from this experience in Joseph's life.

PROSPERITY IS NOT A MATTER OF CIRCUMSTANCES BUT A MATTER OF CHARACTER

At the beginning of Genesis 39, where we are told that Joseph was prosperous and making all around him prosperous as well, where was he? What were his circumstances? He was a piece of human property—the slave of an Egyptian official named Potiphar. At the end of the chapter, he is still prospering, only this time he's in prison.

As Americans—even as American Christians—we have the mistaken notion that prosperity involves some level of material abundance and freedom to do what we want. But in God's eyes, prosperity is a function of character, of being true to God and to His Word. If we are walking faithfully and obediently with God, we can be prosperous in spirit and in character regardless of our circumstances.

Someone from a prior generation wrote this: "God, nothing does, nor suffers to be done, but what we would ourselves, if we could see through all events, or things, as well as He does." In other words, we would put ourselves through the same experiences God allows us to go through if we had God's all-encompassing vantage point on time and history, if we could see the benefits our hard times will produce later. Joseph was a prosperous man because he trusted that God was at work in all the situations in which he found himself.

PERSPECTIVE COMES FROM SEEING GOD IN EVERY CIRCUMSTANCE

It's amazing to see how many times it is said in Genesis 39 that God was with Joseph:

- verse 2: "The Lord was with Joseph"
- verse 3: "The Lord was with him"
- verse 5: "The Lord blessed the Egyptian's house for Joseph's sake"
- verse 21: "But the Lord was with Joseph"
- verse 23: "Because the Lord was with him"

A unique aspect of Christianity is the promise that Christ is with us wherever we go. Our problem is that we forget that He is with us! When difficult times come, we think we are all alone in the midst of our trouble, forgetting that He is right there as well.

The numerous statements of God's presence with Joseph stand in stark contrast to the life of Judah whom we studied in a previous lesson. There is no reference to God being with Judah, because Judah had apparently never been with God. All of Judah's ungodly behavior was a clear indication he felt no accountability at all to the God of his father Jacob. Joseph, on the other hand, seemed to live a life that was sensitive to the presence of God. As a result, God was near to him in everything he did.

It's not hard to see the difference between the two men's lives; and, therefore, it shouldn't be hard to determine which life we would rather live: one where God is "nowhere" or one where God is "now here." The ability to see God in every circumstance comes from first choosing to want God's presence in your life.

PRESENT PROBLEMS OFTEN PREPARE US FOR FUTURE POSITIONS

Joseph didn't know it at the time, but his experience overseeing Potiphar's house and his later assignment to oversee the king's prison were excellent preparation for his eventual promotion to overseeing all of Egypt. In other words, our present assignments, be they good or bad, difficult or easy, often prepare us for future responsibilities.

Joseph was a seventeen-year-old when he had his dreams of his future prominence and prosperity; and not long after that, he arrived in Egypt as a slave. Looking forward a number of years, what would Joseph have known about running an entire country? Nothing, so God sent him to school, first running Potiphar's large household and then running the king's prison. Following those two assignments, Joseph was ready for God's ultimate purpose: to put him in a place of highest authority so he would be able to grant his family safe harbor in Egypt when they came to escape the famine in Canaan.

After graduating from a Christian college and a four-year seminary, and after two years as a pastoral associate, my wife and I started a new church with thirty-two people in the first service—including children and neighbors! I was seriously discouraged. But over the decade we were there, the church grew into a thriving multifaceted ministry; and God gave me every kind of problem any pastor might face. Only when I was invited to the much larger church that I now pastor did I realize how good God's preparation for me had been.

RIGHTEOUSNESS IS NOT ALWAYS IMMEDIATELY REWARDED

Joseph did right in Canaan and was thrown into a pit. He did right in Egypt, and he was thrown into a prison. But God was with him in the pit and the prison. And in due course, God rewarded Joseph's righteousness and faithfulness by elevating him to a place he could never have imagined.

Sometimes we are tempted to get angry or bitter when God seems not to notice that we are trying to live for Him. But when we live for God, especially in the face of persecution, God does see. And the world sees as well. Anybody can fold under pressure, but only the Christian has a reason and the resources to stand firm, knowing that our reward is coming.

So where do you stand with regard to morality—with the new or with the old? Don't let your situation determine your ethics. Instead, live like Joseph: Decide today what you believe and who you represent. Then let your character (Christ in you) shape your response to your circumstances.

APPLICATION

1. To learn about the next difficult trial in Joseph's life, read Genesis 39:13-20.

   a. For what reason are we to do the right thing—to please others and ourselves or to please God?

   b. What did Potiphar's wife accuse Joseph of? (verses 14-15)

   c. When Potiphar's wife told him what happened, what emotion did he convey? (verse 19) At that point, do you think he was more upset at his wife or at Joseph?

   d. What became of Joseph even though he chose to do the right thing for God? (verse 20)

e. Describe a time when you suffered unjustly and how you responded to it. Would your response have been considered praiseworthy before God or not?

2. Read Genesis 39:21-22.

a. While Joseph was in prison, with whom did he gain favor? (verse 21)

b. What character trait did Joseph possess that allowed him to rise to the top in prison?

c. What job did the keeper assign to Joseph? (verse 22)

3. As seen in the trials earlier in Joseph's life, how did the Lord bless all that he did? (verse 23)

   a. What do we, even as Christians, often think of when we think about prosperity?

   b. For what specific reason was Joseph so prosperous? (verses 21 and 23)

   c. How did Joseph's and Judah's lives contrast each other? In order to see God in every circumstance in our lives, what must we do?

d. Based on His promises in Scripture, how confident can you be that God will be with you wherever you go in the future?

4. Turn to the section titled "Present Problems Often Prepare Us for Future Positions."

   a. For what reason do you think God sent Joseph to Egypt to be first a slave and then a prisoner?

   b. What was Joseph's ultimate purpose in Egypt regarding his family?

   c. Do you remember an instance in your life in which you faced multiple trials before reaching God's blessing? If so, was your attitude like Joseph's?

d. As Christians, what reason do we have to stand firm
   amidst trials?

Potiphar's wife referred to Joseph as "the Hebrew servant."
"Hebrew" first occurs in Genesis 14:13 with reference to
"Abram, the Hebrew." It was applied to the descendants of
Abraham, more specifically the descendants of Jacob. Two ideas exist
for the origin of the term. One is that it derives from the name of
Eber, the ancestor of Abraham in Mesopotamia (Genesis 10:21, 24–25).
The other is that the term is related to a Hebrew word meaning
"cross over," referring possibly to the descendants of those who
crossed over either the Euphrates or Jordan rivers on their way
into Canaan. The Greek version of the Old Testament translates
Genesis 14:13 as "Abraham, the one who crossed over" instead of
"Abraham, the Hebrew."

THE ADVANTAGES OF ADVERSITY

Genesis 40:1–23

*In this lesson we discover from the life
of Joseph why troubles can be a good thing.*

OUTLINE

It has been said that trouble doesn't determine character—it reveals it. And for that reason trouble should be seen as a valued friend. It is only during difficulties that we have the chance to see who we really are. Joseph's character was proven during his two years in an Egyptian prison.

  I. Problems Provide Greater Opportunities

 II. Problems Promote Spiritual Maturity

III. Problems Prove Integrity

 IV. Problems Produce a Sense of Dependency

  V. Problems Prepare Our Hearts for Ministry

On November 27, 1965, Howard E. Rutledge parachuted into the hands of the North Vietnamese when his jet fighter was shot down. The story of his subsequent seven-year captivity and torture was popularized several years ago in the best-selling book and movie *In the Presence of Mine Enemies*.

On December 1, he was placed in cell number two in "Heartbreak Hotel," the infamous prison where American POWs were held in Hanoi. He tells in vivid language of the pain of his imprisonment. He writes: "When the door slammed and the key turned in that rusty, iron lock, a feeling of utter loneliness swept over me. I lay down on the cold cement slab in my six-by-six prison. The smell of human excrement burned my nostrils. A rat, as large as a small cat, scampered across the slab beside me. The walls and floors and ceilings were caked with filth. Bars covered a tiny window high above the door. I was cold and hungry. My body ached from swollen joints and sprained muscles.

"It's hard to describe what solitary confinement can do to un-nerve and defeat a man. You quickly tire of standing or of sitting down; sleeping or being awake. There are no books, no papers, no pencils or magazines. The only colors that you see are drab gray and dirty brown. Months or years may go by when you don't see the sunrise or the moon, green grass or flowers. You are locked in, alone and silent in your filthy little cell, breathing stale, rotten air and trying somehow, to keep your sanity."

Whenever we read about an experience like that, the thought immediately comes to mind, "Why would God allow something as evil as this to happen to one of His children? Why would God ever allow such intense pain, or problems of any serious sort, to come to pass in a person's life to the extent that they feared for their very survival?" As Howard Rutledge documents in his book, by the time he was released in 1972, he had learned there are definite advantages to adversity.

And Joseph would learn that as well. We pick up his story after he has been in Egypt for eleven years. In Genesis 37:2, we learn that Joseph was seventeen years old around the time he was sold into slavery; and in 41:46, we learn that he was thirty years old when he became prime minister of Egypt. In Genesis 41:1, we learn that the events of Genesis 40, our text for this lesson, occurred in the two years before he was made prime minister. Therefore, Joseph was around twenty-seven or twenty-eight years old at this point in our story.

The prison in which Joseph was incarcerated was not a prison for common criminals but seems to have been a prison where "royal" prisoners were sent—those who had some connection to the royal court of Pharaoh. For example, the pharaoh's chief butler and baker had also been sent to this prison. All we know as to why they were incarcerated is that "Pharaoh was angry" with them (verse 2).

Joseph noticed one morning that each of the two men had confused, sad looks on their faces. Upon inquiry, he discovered that each man had had a dream the night before that he didn't understand, and there was no one to interpret the dreams. Joseph volunteered to interpret the dreams, telling the men that "interpretations belong to God" (verse 8).

The butler's dream is recorded in verses 9–13. He saw a grape vine with three branches that budded into blossoms and put forth ripe grapes. He saw himself in the dream, taking the grapes and squeezing them into Pharaoh's cup and putting the cup into Pharaoh's hand. Joseph explained that the three branches were three days and that in three days the butler would be restored to his position as Pharaoh's butler.

Hearing the butler's good news, the baker told Joseph his dream (verses 16–19). The baker had seen himself carrying three baskets on his head filled with baked goods for Pharaoh, but there were birds eating the goods that were in the baskets. Joseph had bad news for the baker: Again, "three" represented three days, after which Pharaoh would hang the baker and birds would consume his flesh.

Three days later it happened to be Pharaoh's birthday, and the fate of the butler and baker developed just as Joseph had predicted. But something else more important to Joseph happened when the butler and baker were released. Joseph had asked the butler to put in a good word for him to Pharaoh once he was restored to his former position in Pharaoh's court, to tell Pharaoh that he (Joseph) had done nothing to deserve imprisonment. But once the butler was back in the service of Pharaoh, he failed to do what Joseph had asked (verse 23). Why the butler failed to mention Joseph to Pharaoh is unknown. But we know it resulted in Joseph languishing in prison for two whole years (41:1).

We've seen Joseph be thrown into a pit by his brothers and not complain, and now we see him waiting patiently in prison for two years. In neither case had Joseph done anything wrong, so it was a good opportunity for him to discover God's purpose in these trying circumstances.

I have found five principles in Joseph's response to these circumstances that will help us find the lessons God has for us to learn during times of adversity.

PROBLEMS PROVIDE GREATER OPPORTUNITIES

Did you know there is an entire section of epistles in the New Testament that are referred to as the "prison epistles"? Paul wrote Ephesians, Philippians, Colossians, and Philemon while incarcerated in a Roman prison. The apostle John wrote the book of Revelation while in exile on an island in the Mediterranean Sea. John Bunyan, the author of *Pilgrim's Progress*, wrote his classic allegory while he was in prison. Great things can happen in the midst of adverse circumstances, and Joseph was about to learn that he had not been forgotten by God in his hour of trial. It was a result of his contact in prison with the butler that he would come in contact with Pharaoh, who would put him in the position that led to the fulfillment of his dreams as a teenager.

Charles Colson, the former White House legal counselor to President Nixon, who spent seven months in prison for his part in the Watergate affair, has said that his worst days as a Christian— his prison sentence—were far more rewarding than his best days in the White House. Why? Because prison humbled him and gave him an opportunity to learn to walk with God and learn about the spiritual needs of prisoners. Out of that experience came the Prison Fellowship ministry that has reached so many prisoners with the Gospel as well as ministered to their families.

Yes, adversities are difficult. But they often contain opportunities we would not have discovered without going through the trouble.

PROBLEMS PROMOTE SPIRITUAL MATURITY

Problems have the potential to make us better or to make us bitter. It is up to us to decide what the result of problems in our life will be. If we refuse to become bitter in the midst of problems, by default we will become better.

Few people in Scripture experienced more unfair treatment than Joseph. He was obedient to his father to go and check on his brothers and was thrown in a pit and sold as a slave as a result. He kept his morality and would not succumb to Mrs. Potiphar's temptations in Egypt and was thrown into prison as a result. In prison he faithfully interpreted his friend's dream and was then ignored by the man he helped. No matter what Joseph did, he received only pain and misery for his trouble. But Joseph never complained.

It is likely that Joseph lived a privileged life growing up. His brothers worked hard tending the flocks while Joseph stayed home and wore his favorite-son robe. Joseph needed to be toughened up if he was going to assume the leadership of Egypt during a great famine and make a way of deliverance for his family. Joseph went into his difficult experiences as an undisciplined man but came out as a mature man. His soul was toughened, made mature, by the iron that bound him in prison (Psalm 105:17–18). He gained wisdom and a deeper perspective; he became a man suited to lead a nation.

God needs the same kind of people today, and the only way we will gain Joseph's maturity is to respond to trouble like Joseph did. God makes us strong through suffering. In today's church, the doctrine that God wants you to be rich and comfortable is being taught. But that is not the doctrine of the New Testament. Every person who was used significantly by God in the New Testament, including Jesus Christ Himself, was severely tested and poor for the sake of the Gospel. The idea that we will go through the spiritual life without experiencing trouble and affliction is a false doctrine.

God used affliction to make Joseph into a man qualified for new dimensions of leadership and service, and He will do the same with us.

PROBLEMS PROVE INTEGRITY

Nothing tests our character like adversity. When circumstances are going our way, it's easy to act spiritually mature. It's when life turns against us that we are called upon to demonstrate that our character is genuine. As has been said by many, adversity doesn't produce character—it reveals it.

Character is often confused with reputation, but there is a big difference. Reputation is what others think we are, whereas character is what we really are. Reputation is what men think you are, whereas character is what God knows you are. Reputation is what is chiseled on your tombstone, whereas character is what the angels say about you before the throne of God. Reputation may change with circumstances or the seasons of life, whereas character should never change.

For those reasons, we should welcome problems when they come because they give us a chance to see for ourselves who we really are. Again, when things are going well, that is not the complete picture of our character. We need both good times and hard times to get the full picture. In that way, problems prove integrity.

PROBLEMS PRODUCE A SENSE OF DEPENDENCY

We have already seen in previous lessons how the Lord was with Joseph in prison (Genesis 39:20–21), showing that it is not circumstances that separate us from the Lord, but sin. Walking in righteousness and purity keeps our fellowship with God intact, but sin breaks that relationship. Even if we are in prison or in some other difficult circumstance, God remains with us if we remain with God.

W. H. Griffith-Thomas wrote these words to show the relationship between Joseph's power and God's presence: "The secret of Joseph's power was the consciousness of the presence of God. God had not forgotten him, though it might have seemed to him that it was the case. The very incident that was apparently the most injurious was the link used by God to bring about Joseph's exaltation. To the man who is sure that he is in the pathway of God's will, there will come the consciousness of the divine presence and blessing which will be an unspeakable comfort as he rests in the Lord and waits patiently for Him. Evil may have its temporary victories, but they are only temporary. Good and right and truth must prevail, and it is for the servants of God to wait quietly, to go forward humbly, to live faithfully, and to trust boldly until God shall justify them by His divine interposition and glorify His grace in their lives."

We never have as deep a sense of God's love for us as when we are in troubling times. I have had many, many people tell me through the years, in the midst of difficult times, something like this: "Pastor, I knew that God loved me, and I've always felt close to Him, but I have never in my life known the fellowship that I have known while in this pressure cooker. God has been with me." We need problems in our lives to show us how dependent we are upon the Lord and to remind us that the do-it-yourself and sustain-yourself culture we live in is not biblical when it comes to spiritual strength.

PROBLEMS PREPARE OUR HEARTS FOR MINISTRY

Joseph was in prison unjustly and encountered two of his fellow prisoners who were obviously troubled (40:6–7). Instead of being absorbed in his own situation and groveling in self-pity, Joseph took the opportunity to minister to the two men who were in need of help. Joseph didn't think God had abandoned him in light of his circumstances. In fact, he was so confident of God's presence that he felt sure God would give to him the interpretations of the men's dreams.

There is no ministry to those who are suffering like the ministry given by another sufferer. That is exactly what Paul referred to in 2 Corinthians 1 when he said, ". . . we may be able to comfort those who are in any trouble, with the comfort with which we ourselves are comforted by God" (verse 4). Suffering makes you able to reach out with authenticity to comfort others who are suffering. How can we reach out to others who are hurting if we ourselves have never experienced the grace of God in our own times of suffering? We cannot say, "I know how you feel," if we have not felt the same kind of pain that others have felt.

I remember the first funeral I performed as an associate pastor fresh out of seminary. It was for a couple who lost their little ten-month-old baby. Just four months before that happened, my wife had miscarried her first pregnancy, which was devastating for us since we had been trying for several years to start a family. In no way was the loss of our baby equal to the pain of our friends in losing their ten-month-old. But in some small way, we were able to identify with what they felt as a result of our own experience.

Howard Rutledge, the Vietnam POW, had his life changed by his years of suffering in prison. He learned the power of prayer and the omnipresence of God. He realized how he had excluded God from his life and made a commitment to confess his faith in Christ and join his family in church membership. And he resolved never to be without a copy of the Bible again.

If you are not in a difficult place right now, you likely will be in the future. Look for the reasons God has you there, and the experience will make you better instead of bitter.

1. Turn to Genesis 40:1-23 to read about the advantages of adversity in Joseph's life.

    a. Who was thrown into the prison where Joseph was confined? Why did they end up there? (verses 2-3)

    b. When Joseph came to these two men one morning, for what reason were they sad? (verses 7-8)

    c. When Joseph volunteered to interpret their dreams, what did he tell the men? (verse 8)

    d. Explain the butler's dream as recorded in verses 9-11. What did Joseph's interpretation consist of? (verses 12-13)

e. When the baker told Joseph his dream, how was it interpreted? (verses 16-19) Did these dreams come true just as Joseph said they would? (verses 20-22)

f. What did Joseph ask the butler to do once released from prison? Did he honor that request? (verses 14-15, 23)

2. Joseph never complained about his circumstances—no matter what they were.

a. God used _____ to turn Joseph into a more qualified man for the position of leadership. ("Problems Promote Spiritual Maturity")

b. Compare and contrast Joseph's difficult circumstances to a difficult circumstance in your own life. Can you spot any differences in the way you handled the situation compared to Joseph?

c. Once that difficult situation was over, were you able to understand God's purpose for it?

3. Turn to the section titled "Problems Prove Integrity."

a. _____ is what men think you are, and _____ is what God knows you are.

b. Does adversity produce character or reveal it? Should one's character change? Why or why not?

c. Why should we be aware of and open to problems? What do they prove?

4. In the midst of difficult circumstances, what happens if we remain close to God?

a. Why is it necessary for us to undergo trials in life?

b. Have you ever felt as if you could handle a problem by yourself? If you tried this "do-it-yourself" method, what was the end result?

5. Turn to "Problems Prepare Our Hearts for Ministry."

a. Instead of sitting in his self-pity, how did Joseph react to the situation that lay before him in prison?

b. What is Paul's message to those who have encountered tribulation? (2 Corinthians 1:4)

c. Why might our own suffering be a benefit to others who are suffering?

DID YOU KNOW?

John Bunyan's *Pilgrim's Progress from This World to That Which Is to Come* was published in 1678 (part one) and 1684 (part two). He wrote it while in prison, having been incarcerated in 1675 for violating the Conventicle Act which punished Englishmen for conducting religious services outside the Church of England. It is said to be the second best-selling book in history after the Bible, having been translated into more than 100 languages. It is considered to be not only a classic of Christian literature but of literature in general. It is often the first book missionaries translate after translating the Bible.

FROM PRISON TO PALACE

Genesis 41:1–45

*In this lesson we discover how and why
God accomplished His will in Joseph's life.*

OUTLINE

Many Christians focus a lot of spiritual and emotional energy on discerning the will of God for their lives. Joseph focused mainly on being faithful in the moment, leaving the long-range details to God. As a result, God's perfect will for Joseph's life, and Jacob's family, was accomplished.

  I. **The Ways of God**

 II. **The Wisdom of God**
    A. Perfect Timing
    B. Perfect Tactics

III. **The Will of God**
    A. Present Joseph to Pharaoh
    B. Predict Egypt's Future
    C. Propose a Solution
    D. Promote Joseph to Prime Minister

IV. **Joseph's Responsibility**
    A. Courageous Vision
    B. Committed to God's Glory
    C. Controlled by the Holy Spirit
    D. Cooperative With God's Process of Training

In her book, *Triumph for God*, Corrie ten Boom describes what her feelings were the day she was miraculously released from a Nazi concentration prison camp: "One week before the order came to kill all of the women my age, I was free. I still do not understand all the details of my release from Ravensbrook; all I know is, it was a miracle of God. The gate swung open, and I glimpsed the lake in front of the camp. I could smell freedom. 'Follow me' a young girl said in an officer's uniform. I walked slowly through the gate, never looking back. Behind me I heard the hinges squeak as the gate swung shut. I was free! And flooding through my mind were the words of Jesus to the church of Philadelphia: 'Behold I have sent before thee an open door, and no man can shut it.'"

Surely something similar to Corrie ten Boom's emotions must have flooded the heart and mind of Joseph the day he walked out of the king's prison in Egypt. After two long years, he was free. In this situation, which we will study in this lesson, we see again the two parallel tracks that seem to define Joseph's life: God's providence and Joseph's personal choices to make decisions that cooperated fully with God's providence.

Theologians have debated forever the tension between God's sovereignty and man's responsibility. In truth, the tension exists only on earth. We may not fully understand the harmony between the two in heaven, but it is there. As God acts and man acts, the two coincide at every point to accomplish the purposes of God. Man is never free to abdicate his responsibility, saying, "God's going to do what He wants anyway." Man is always held responsible, which makes Joseph's actions so commendable. In spite of the difficulties he went through, he always chose to honor God in his actions. Joseph is a beautiful study in the providence of God and the responsibility of man.

THE WAYS OF GOD

While Joseph was in prison, God was at work. We don't know why Joseph had to languish in captivity for two years; but when the time came for him to be released, he was. To be honest, we have to note that Joseph tried to help God out when he asked the butler to put in a good word for him to Pharaoh, which the butler didn't do. Was Joseph trying to take matters into his own hands and speed up the process? It's hard to say. I don't see his action as anything more than anyone would do. Nonetheless, it had no impact on God's timetable. The day Joseph was released, it was obvious that God had orchestrated it, not man.

After Joseph had been in prison two years (Genesis 41:1), Pharaoh had a dream. In his dream he was standing by the Nile River when he saw seven fat, well-fed cows come up out of the river and begin to feed in a meadow. Then seven thin, starving cows came up out of the river and ate up the seven fat, sleek cows. Apparently startled by the dream, Pharaoh awoke but fell asleep again, whereupon he had a second dream.

The second dream was about ears of corn. Seven fat, plump ears appeared on a single stalk, followed by seven dry, wasted ears on another stalk. The seven wasted ears devoured the seven plump ears. And Pharaoh woke up a second time.

Dreams were important in Egyptian culture—a medium for messages from their gods. To receive two startling dreams in one night, both so similar—sets of impoverished sevens destroying sets of abundant sevens—troubled Pharaoh greatly. He personally didn't understand the message of the dreams, so he called in "all the magicians of Egypt and all its wise men" (verse 8) to seek the answer. But they were clueless as to the dreams' meanings. These dreams were from God, and there was no way these men who didn't know God could receive the interpretation from Him.

At this point, God's divine connections come into play. The butler, who had been in prison with Joseph, remembered that Joseph had correctly interpreted his and the baker's dreams. And he recommended Joseph to Pharaoh—exactly what Joseph had asked him to do many months before, though for a different reason. Pharaoh took the butler's advice and called Joseph from prison to interpret his dreams.

The path was circuitous and time-consuming, but God's ways resulted in Joseph being released from prison at a time that would see him elevated to a place of high authority in Egypt.

THE WISDOM OF GOD

The ways of God always reflect the wisdom of God—His timing and "tactics" are always perfect.

Perfect Timing

At the very moment Pharaoh had a need that no one in his royal court could meet, the only man in the world who knew Joseph could interpret dreams was standing right there. (Remember, Pharaoh had the baker killed, which left only the butler who knew Joseph and his "gift.") A number of different things had to have happened in order to bring Joseph face-to-face with the pharaoh of Egypt—and they all happened:

1. Potiphar's wife had to accuse Joseph wrongly.

2. Joseph had to be sent to prison.

3. The keeper of the prison had to like Joseph and give him free access throughout the prison.

4. Pharaoh's butler and baker had to be put in prison.

5. Joseph had to meet them and be there the day they were both disconcerted about their dreams.

6. Joseph had to be able to interpret their dreams.

7. The butler had to remember that experience for nearly two years.

8. The butler had to be present the day Pharaoh's dreams went uninterpreted.

9. Pharaoh had to be willing to bring a prisoner into his court to try to interpret his dreams.

10. Joseph had to receive the interpretation of Pharaoh's dreams from God.

Like clockwork, the pieces of this puzzle fell into place all at the right time.

Perfect Tactics

How would you get the most powerful ruler in the world at that time to listen to God? The way God did it was to give him a problem he couldn't solve through his normal methods. So God gave Pharaoh two dreams that troubled him so deeply that he was willing to listen to a prisoner who claimed his God could interpret them. God's ways of orchestrating events are always subtly amazing.

When we would do door-to-door evangelism years ago, we would make return visits to homes where people had not been interested in receiving Christ. (If they specifically asked us not to return, we honored that request.) I once visited a man in his home seven times over a long period of time, and he became a Christian on the seventh visit. I can't explain that other than to say the events that had transpired in his life by the seventh visit made him ready to listen to the Gospel and embrace it. Those events are the "tactics" of God—the things He does in His perfect time and way to bring about the consummation of His will.

THE WILL OF GOD

The ways of God and the wisdom of God always combine to result in the will of God being accomplished.

Present Joseph to Pharaoh

Think of the beginning and end of God's will in the grand scheme of things. The beginning is to preserve the family of Jacob through whom the promises of Abraham will be fulfilled. The end is to isolate Jacob's family in a protected environment so they can grow into a nation for 430 years. Based on where we are in that story, the next step is to present Joseph to Pharaoh so Joseph might eventually get the kind of influence in Egypt that will allow him to secure a refuge for his (Jacob's) family.

One minute Joseph is in prison, and the next minute he's standing before Pharaoh. The will of God is being accomplished.

Predict Egypt's Future

A substep in the working out of God's will is for Joseph to interpret Pharaoh's two dreams—necessary in order for Pharaoh to see Joseph's wisdom and appoint him to a place of authority in Egypt.

Joseph summarized by explaining that Pharaoh had only one dream, not two, meaning there was only one message but shown in two different ways (verses 25, 32). In Egyptian culture, the doubling or repetition of a dream meant that the message was important and was about to happen. So Joseph had Pharaoh's undivided attention.

You can read Joseph's detailed explanations in verses 25–32, but here's the summary: Egypt is about to experience seven years of plenty followed by seven years of famine. Not just famine, but a very severe famine that could wipe out all of Egypt's reserves and prosperity. All of this has been "established by God," Joseph said (verse 32), so it's time to prepare.

Propose a Solution

The third part of God's will was to have Joseph propose a solution to Pharaoh. Here's a man fresh out of prison who not only has told the most powerful man in the world that his country is facing perilous times, he also proposes a solution (verses 33–36). Joseph isn't auditioning for a job here, he's just trying to help Pharaoh get started preparing for the coming crisis. Joseph suggests appointing someone to administer the following program: Store up 20 percent of Egypt's output of grain and produce for the next seven years, and then use those reserves to live off of during the seven years of famine. Pharaoh liked the idea so much that he appointed Joseph to head up the program.

Promote Joseph to Prime Minister

Because it was God's will to bring Joseph's family to Egypt, it's obvious that it was His will to put Joseph in a position to make that happen. So Joseph was made the new prime minister of Egypt (verses 37–45). In Middle Eastern cultures, there was an officer called the vizier whose power and authority went far beyond what we might refer to as the prime minister. And Joseph became Pharaoh's vizier. This meant he was consulted on every matter of importance to come before Pharaoh; and in Pharaoh's absence, Joseph could rule with the full authority of Pharaoh behind his decisions. In essence, he was the most powerful man in Egypt next to Pharaoh and was almost as powerful as the pharaoh himself.

With his promotion there would have been a number of rewards accruing to Joseph in his new position. First, Pharaoh gave him his own signet ring that served as an official stamp on government documents (verse 42). Anything Joseph sealed with this ring bore the authority of Pharaoh.

Second, Joseph was given garments of fine linen to wear. Joseph began with the special robe that helped arouse his brothers' jealousy, then he wore the robe of a servant in Potiphar's household where he was thrown in jail. And now he has the royal robe of the Pharaoh, a robe he would not lose for the next eighty years.

Third, he received a gold chain from Pharaoh to wear around his neck, likely a symbol of his wealth, status, and authority in Egypt.

Fourth, Joseph was given a chariot to ride in directly behind Pharaoh's chariot as they went about the land.

Finally, Pharaoh issued a decree that all the nation should pay homage to Joseph when he passed by. In Egypt, rulers were considered to be gods, so this was an act of worship. One of Joseph's original dreams had his family bowing down to him, which would soon happen. But in addition, all the nation of Egypt was bowing down as well.

Not only did Joseph receive rewards, there were good reasons for why the rewards should have been given.

JOSEPH'S RESPONSIBILITY

There were four reasons God promoted Joseph to be the virtual ruler of the most powerful nation on earth. And these are qualities we should look for in our own lives as we seek to be used by the Lord.

Courageous Vision

First, Joseph had a courageous vision. Joseph paid a price for the vision God gave him in his dreams; but he never lost the vision, not even through 12 years of testing in the crucible of suffering and disappointment. Someone has said that the true test of a vision is whether we are easily discouraged from pursuing it. Using that test, Joseph's vision was definitely a valid one since he never gave up on it.

Committed to God's Glory

Second, Joseph was committed to God's glory. The reason God blessed Joseph's vision was that Joseph remained committed to God's glory in the pursuit of the vision. When Joseph stood before Pharaoh to interpret his dreams, he told Pharaoh that he did not have the ability to interpret the dreams but God did (verses 16, 25, 28, 32). As badly as Joseph wanted to get out of prison, he refused to take credit for something that only God could do. God will bless a person with that kind of honesty, humility, and integrity.

Controlled by the Holy Spirit

Third, Joseph was controlled by the Holy Spirit. Even Pharaoh noticed that Joseph was no ordinary man—that the Spirit of God dwelled in him, giving him the power to interpret dreams that no human could interpret (verse 38). Obviously, Pharaoh didn't mean by his words what we mean when we refer to the Spirit of God. He simply meant that Joseph demonstrated a supernatural quality to his life that others didn't possess. Joseph's calm stability, his confidence, his character—all these qualities set him apart. We hear much today about being Spirit-filled and the power of supernatural gifts and the working of miracles. Without taking issue with those beliefs, we can also say that in the New Testament, being Spirit-filled is also associated with living faithfully in everyday circumstances (Ephesians 5:18 ff.). Joseph didn't work any miracles in Egypt, but he definitely lived a godly, practical life as observed by others.

Cooperative With God's Process of Training

Fourth, Joseph cooperated with God's training program for his life. God gave Joseph eighty years of ministry in Egypt with only 13 years of training. Throughout those years, in whatever situation he found himself, Joseph was a faithful student. He took whatever God gave him and learned the lesson. From Joseph we learn the lesson that it is not our circumstances that are important. It is who we are! Whether Joseph was in the pit, Potiphar's house, Pharaoh's prison, or the palace, he was faithfully the same in all four situations. God's men and women don't ask God to change their circumstances, they ask God to change them in the midst of the circumstances.

God is looking for more Josephs, more men and women to pursue a courageous vision for God's glory, who are filled with the Spirit and receive the training God gives them. Is that you?

APPLICATION

1. Turn to Genesis 41:1-45 to read how God accomplished His will in Joseph's life.

   a. After two years passed, and Joseph was still in prison, who had a dream that needed interpreting? (verse 1)

   b. How many dreams did he have? Write a brief summary. (verses 2-7)

   c. According to Egyptian culture, why were dreams so important? ("The Ways of God")

   d. When Pharaoh woke up after a troubling night's sleep, whom did he call for to interpret his dreams? Were they able to determine the meaning? (verse 8)

   e. No one could understand what Pharaoh's dreams meant. What do you think God's reasoning was for this?

   f. Who spoke up, remembering it was Joseph who interpreted his dream with accuracy? (verses 9-13)

2. Turn to the section titled "The Wisdom of God."

   a. Name a few of the different events that took place leading up to Joseph's face-to-face encounter with Pharaoh.

   b. When Joseph responded to Pharaoh's request for interpretation, what did he tell him? (verses 15-16)

3. Turn to verses 25-32 to read Joseph's interpretation of Pharaoh's dream.

   a. Summarize Joseph's explanation of the events that would take place in the near future, according to his interpretation.

   b. In verses 33-36, Joseph established a plan for Pharaoh in order to protect Egypt from the coming famine. Who did he advise Pharaoh to appoint to be head of that plan?

4. Read verses 37-45 to see God's will continue to play out in Joseph's life.

   a. After Pharaoh agreed to appoint someone over the land of Egypt, what was he unsure of? (verse 38)

b. What became of Joseph? Why did Pharaoh believe he would be best for the job? (verse 39)

c. With power came reward. What did Pharaoh give to Joseph as a sign of his new authority? ("Promote Joseph to Prime Minister")

5. God allowed Joseph to be promoted because he possessed certain qualities that made him suitable for the job. List these qualities.

a. He had a _____ vision.

b. He was _____ to God's glory.

c. He was _____ by the Holy Spirit.

6. Using Joseph as an example, how does loyalty translate into life? How does a person loyal to God act, especially when under pressure or difficulty?

a. In what way should being "filled with the Spirit" (Ephesians 5:18) be evident to non-Christians?

b. What aspects of your life most evidence "the Spirit of God"? What aspects should reveal more of God's presence than they do?

The debate between God's sovereignty and man's responsibility is referred to by philosophers and theologians as an antinomy (an-tí-no-mee). Antinomy comes from the Greek *anti* (against) and *nomos* (law) and pictures two laws being against, or contradictory to, one another. Practically, it suggests a situation in which two laws are mutually exclusive or mutually incompatible—both cannot be true at the same time. The laws represent a paradox, an unresolved contradiction. But the Bible teaches both: the sovereignty of God (Psalm 115:3; Daniel 4:35; Ephesians 1:11) and the responsibility of man (Acts 16:31; Romans 10:9). The truths only conflict from a human point of view, not from God's (Isaiah 55:8–9).

JOSEPH THE PRIME MINISTER

Genesis 41:37–57

*In this lesson we learn about the ministry
God gave Joseph in Egypt.*

OUTLINE

Part of the unbiblical sacred/secular dichotomy is the idea that ministers in the church are those who bear the title. The biblical truth is that every Christian is a minister. The story of Joseph in Egypt shows how God providentially prepares a ministry for those who live in His will.

I. God's Preparation for Ministry
  A. Progressively Increased Responsibility
  B. Progressively Increased Difficulty

II. God's Personal Provision for Ministry
  A. Family in the Midst of Foreigners
  B. Food in the Midst of Famine
  C. Faith in the Midst of Fear

III. God's Providential Plan for Ministry
  A. The Immediate Plan
  B. The Ultimate Plan

IV. God's Practical Advice for Ministry
  A. For Sufferers
  B. For Servants

W e are using the phrase "prime minister" to describe the position to which Joseph has ascended in his sudden promotion from prison to the palace of Pharaoh. Taken from prison, washed, shaved, clothed in clean garments, this Hebrew slave is brought before Pharaoh and is suddenly appointed and anointed to be Pharaoh's vice-ruler of all of Egypt. Could this have happened any other way except by God's providential plan being active in Joseph's life?

But it's clear that God has more in store for Joseph than being a political figure in Egypt—a prime minister. Actually, God has called Joseph to this lofty position to be a minister—to serve not only his own family but to serve the people of Egypt as well. A great famine is about to come upon Egypt; and God, in an act of grace, has put Joseph in a place to save the entire nation. Just as God's blessing extended to Potiphar's household when Joseph worked there, so now God's blessing will extend to the entire nation as a result of Joseph's promotion.

From Joseph's preparation and appointment, we can glean insights about what it takes to be a faithful minister: God's preparation, provision, and plan.

GOD'S PREPARATION FOR MINISTRY

The methods God uses to train His ministers are unique—a progressive increase in responsibility and difficulty.

Progressively Increased Responsibility

In Genesis 41:41, Pharaoh put Joseph in charge of "all the land of Egypt." But Joseph certainly did not start there; he didn't go from being a seventeen-year-old in Canaan to prime minister of Egypt overnight. Instead, God sent Joseph through the school of "progressively increased responsibility."

Three times we find Joseph's responsibility being increased:

- Genesis 39:4 - Joseph was made overseer of Potiphar's house in which he was a servant.
- Genesis 39:22 - Joseph was made overseer of the prison where he was incarcerated.
- Genesis 41:41 - Joseph was made overseer of all the land of Egypt.

Joseph was living out the principle expressed by Jesus Christ in Luke 16:10, that "he who is faithful in what is least is faithful also in much." Responsibility is given progressively by God; and when it is fulfilled, more is given. What is important in God's sight is not our position or place but our faithfulness, our willingness to take whatever assignment God gives us and do it in a way that honors Him.

Young people make the mistake of believing they are entitled to inherit the standard of living they grew up with when they go out on their own. They forget that their parents have already worked twenty or thirty years to achieve what they have and that they (the young people) will have to do the same. Anyone who wants God's blessing in his life in the future needs to ask, "What has God given me to do today—and how well am I doing it?" Working for God today with our whole heart is the key to God's blessing tomorrow (Colossians 3:23).

Progressively Increased Difficulty

Increased responsibility leads to the second reality: increased difficulty. Increased success in life follows the shape of a pyramid. More people drop out as the difficulty increases; those willing to accept the increased difficulty are fewer and fewer the higher up one goes on the pyramid of success.

To that end, A. W. Tozer has written, "The devil, things, and people being what they are, it's necessary to use the hammer, the file and the furnace in the holy work of preparing the saint for saint-hood. It is doubtful whether God can bless a man greatly until He has hurt him deeply." Naturally speaking, most people (including me) recoil at such a thought. We want to be comfortable in life, but we also want to be blessed by God. Tozer says blessing only comes with increased difficulty, which usually leads to increased discomfort.

Joseph's difficulty certainly increased. Thrown in a pit, then thrown in jail. Being accused of egotism, then accused of sexual assault. Betrayed by a friend who was supposed to help him get out of jail, he was left in jail for two years though innocent all the while. For eleven years Joseph experienced increasing difficulty which he willingly accepted. But there was a purpose in Joseph's preparation. Four hundred thirty years later, another Hebrew came on the scene to lead Jacob's family back to Canaan—Moses, who had spent eighty years in preparation for his task. God doesn't use anybody whom He doesn't first prepare.

GOD'S PERSONAL PROVISION FOR MINISTRY

God cares for us personally at the same time He prepares us for ministry. In Joseph's case, God gave him a family in a foreign land, food in the midst of a famine, and faith in the midst of fear.

Family in the Midst of Foreigners

Joseph was isolated in Egypt, an island in an ocean of foreigners. In time, God provided a wife and children for Joseph to give his life a measure of normalcy and support (verses 45, 50). Joseph was given an Egyptian name and a wife who was the daughter of an Egyptian priest in the city of On, a city where festivals were held in honor of the sun god. Pharaoh was thought to be the incarnation of the sun god, a deity walking on earth. For Joseph to marry this priest's daughter made them Egypt's premier power couple.

The question can be raised about Joseph marrying a pagan, an unbeliever. But we have to remember that the Mosaic Laws and New Testament admonitions about not being yoked together with unbelievers are far into the future. This was no different than Isaac and Jacob marrying women from among their original cultural settings in terms of faith. The only woman in Jacob's family to marry would have been Dinah, Joseph's sister, which was obviously not an option.

This was clearly a transitional time in the plan of God when Jacob's family was being sent to Egypt to be developed into a nation. Once the nation was large enough to gain size and strength in Egypt, there would be less marrying of outsiders (Genesis 43:32; 46:34). But for now, Joseph needed a wife and family, and God provided that for him in Egypt—two good "things" (Proverbs 18:22; Psalm 127:3–5). Joseph named his sons Manasseh ("forget"), the firstborn, and Ephraim ("twice fruitful") (verses 51–52). His two sons were reminders of how God had blessed him and helped him forget his former toil and how God had made him fruitful in the land of his affliction, the land of Egypt. With one son came the healing of many painful memories; and with the second, a fresh sense of fruitfulness in his life. God gave Joseph what he would need to make a home in Egypt since he would spend the rest of his life there.

Food in the Midst of Famine

Let's use the split-screen, or picture-in-picture, approach to this next provision of God. In Canaan, picture Jacob and his family out of the will of God as they get involved in one debacle after another. In Egypt is Joseph, in the will of God, moving up steadily in his responsibility as a leader and minister in this foreign land. Then, covering both screens, comes a famine that affects both Canaan and Egypt. Jacob and his family in Canaan are starving, while Joseph and his family and all the Egyptians have food under the direction of Joseph who has stockpiled enough reserves to see them through (verses 47, 49).

Joseph is in the will of God in a foreign land that he went to involuntarily—and prospering—while Jacob's family is living out of the will of God in their homeland—and starving. The moral of that story is that you are better off in the will of God regardless of where God's will takes you. Where God's will is, there is the provision of God.

Faith in the Midst of Fear

As Joseph got promoted up the ladder of responsibility and authority in Egypt, he did not forget his God. The name that Pharaoh gave to Joseph (Zaphnath-paaneah), as well as the name of his wife (Asenath), both contained the letters "n-a-t-h." In Egypt this was a name for "god." It seemed that Pharaoh recognized Joseph as a "man of God" (41:38) and so gave him a new name, and a wife with a name, that would acknowledge Joseph's godliness. Joseph was different from the Egyptians, and Pharaoh honored that by acknowledging his "religion." When Joseph and his wife had children, they were given Hebrew names straight out of Joseph's culture.

So Joseph maintained his spiritual integrity and his ties to his own religious culture even though he was as deeply assimilated into Egyptian culture as he could possibly be. In a land where he was the only person who worshiped Jehovah-God, Joseph kept his faith intact. God never left Joseph, and Joseph never left God.

GOD'S PROVIDENTIAL PLAN FOR MINISTRY

There were two aspects to the ministry God had planned for Joseph: an immediate plan and an ultimate plan.

The Immediate Plan

The immediate plan was to put Joseph in a place of administrative authority in Egypt so he could provide food for a hungry nation. I see six principles at work in God's immediate plan for Joseph.

1. Personal Inspection

Verse 45 indicates that as soon as he was given his new position of responsibility by Pharaoh, Joseph traveled all over Egypt. His mission was probably to assess the food situation in terms of implementing the plan he recommended to Pharaoh. Joseph was obviously a hands-on leader, getting to know the land and the people who would provide the resources for the next seven years to avert a famine in Egypt for the following seven years.

2. Central Administration

Verses 34 and 35 indicate a top-down approach to saving Egypt from the approaching famine. The project would be "under the authority of Pharaoh" but administered by Joseph. All the land would be involved. Joseph had centralized control over the project and expected the whole country to participate in the coming seven years of setting aside resources.

3. Disciplined Conservation

Verse 48 says Joseph "gathered up all the food of the seven years" in Egypt to store it up for the coming years of shortages. Like the ant in Proverbs 6 that works hard in the summer to store up food supplies for the winter, so Joseph led the nation in a disciplined program of saving, something every person and nation should practice.

4. Local Distribution

While the program of saving was administered centrally from Joseph's "office," it was implemented locally. Joseph's advice to Pharaoh was to "let them keep food in the cities" (verse 35). Grow the food locally, store it locally, and ultimately dispense it locally. And that is what they did: They "laid up in every city the food of the fields which surrounded them" (verse 48). This would be the equivalent in the United States of having a federal program in place but having it implemented at the state level.

5. Economic Consideration

Joseph was a brilliant manager. After the seven years of famine were over, Egypt was probably in the best financial condition it had ever been in. Why? Because Joseph had grain reserves to sell to all the nations surrounding Egypt that were struck by the famine. While it may seem harsh on Joseph's part to sell the grain instead of giving it away, the text doesn't say the people were out of money. Nor does it say Joseph took advantage of their situation. Egypt had worked hard to prepare for the worst, and they were rewarded for their efforts by making a profit from their labors. It would have been out of character for Joseph to have taken advantage of the Egyptians or those from other countries, and I doubt if he did. Joseph was amazing in many respects: leader, spiritually-sensitive, good businessman—the blessings of God were abundant in his life.

6. Worldwide Recognition

Joseph's wisdom and discernment, given by God, made Egypt the preeminent nation in the world. They were the only ones with food among those nations affected by the famine. Because Joseph lived in the will of God, he was able to lead Egypt into a place of blessing. One of the signs of God's blessing—one of the characteristics He intended for Israel to be known for—is having enough to meet the needs of others and a willingness to do so. Joseph turned Egypt, for seven years, into a nation that fed the world. God intended for Israel to play that same role, but unfortunately she lived too much out of the will of God.

The Ultimate Plan

Feeding Israel and the nations of the world was an immediate benefit of God's plan for Joseph, but it was not the ultimate benefit. The ultimate plan is noted in Genesis 42:1–2: to have a place where Joseph's own family, the family of Jacob, inheritor of the promises of Abraham, could find shelter from the moral and agricultural famine in Canaan. Of the 13 famines mentioned in the Bible, this one seems to have been orchestrated by God for the express purpose of driving Jacob's family down to Egypt where they would be secluded and protected until they were large enough to develop enough spiritual, national, and religious momentum to carry them into the future.

Jacob's family's existence in Canaan was tenuous at best. Numbering only seventy-odd, they would have been easy prey for the Canaanites militarily. And they could easily have found themselves assimilated into the immoral culture of Canaan and lost their focus as the channel of God's covenant promises and blessings as given to Abraham. So God took them to Egypt where Jacob's son, Joseph, could give them refuge. That was God's ultimate plan, worked out through the life of Joseph.

God's Practical Advice for Ministry

Jacob was both a sufferer and a servant, and we can find applications for ourselves from both aspects of his life.

For Sufferers

God can help us forget our past hurts and pains. We may not have suffered like Joseph, but we have pain from the past in one form or another. God can give you the name Manasseh as He makes you forget all the pain of your past. And He can give you the name Ephraim as He restores fruitfulness to what has been a barren field. God did that for Joseph and can do the same for you.

For Servants

For all who are called to serve God in some way—and every Christian is—we learn from Joseph's life that God always provides for those whose service is in the will of God. It is better to be in the will of God obediently in a distant land than to be out of the will of God in your own home.

I pray you are challenged by the life of Joseph, whether suffering or serving, to live patiently and faithfully in God's providential will for your life.

1. Read Genesis 41:37-57 to learn about Joseph's journey to becoming a faithful minister.

   a. In what three instances can we find Joseph's responsibility increase?

      • Genesis 39:4

      • Genesis 39:22

      • Genesis 41:41

   b. What happens when we fulfill the responsibilities in our lives? Why are we to be ready and willing to take on any assignment God gives us?

   c. How do you feel about what God has given you to do? In what ways do you wish it were "greater"?

d. How would you assess your faithfulness in carrying out your present "assignment(s)"?

2. Turn to the section "God's Personal Provision for Ministry."

   a. In the midst of Joseph's preparation for ministry, what (whom) did God provide for him? (verses 45 and 50)

   b. Although Joseph's wife was a pagan, why did God incorporate their marriage into His plan for Joseph's life?

   c. Compare and contrast Joseph's life in Egypt with his family's life in Canaan. What went on in Egypt that contributed to their prosperity during the famine compared to that of Canaan? (verses 47-49)

d. What new name did Pharaoh give to Joseph? What was his wife's name? (verse 45) How did this indicate that Joseph was being assimilated into the Egyptian culture?

3. God had an immediate and an ultimate plan for Joseph.

   a. The first step of the immediate plan involved what, according to verse 45?

   b. Joseph's discipline led to his conservation. In verse 48, what did he gather up to be saved for seven years? How much did he gather? (verse 49)

   c. The ability to manage and conserve helped Joseph be successful. What character traits did God give Joseph that helped make Egypt such a dominant nation? (See "Worldwide Recognition.")

d. What was God's ultimate plan for Joseph's family? (See Genesis 42:1-2.) What was the purpose behind this plan?

4. What character traits has God given you that have helped you prosper, despite the circumstances surrounding you?

a. What have you learned from how Joseph multiplied his possibilities as a slave for Potiphar and then as a prisoner?

b. Instead of advancing and doing his best, what might he have done (motivated by self-pity or resentment toward God)?

Because the biblical story played out in the generally arid Middle East, food and water were a continual challenge. As a result, famines and droughts represented major threats to survival. Death by the sword was preferable to death by famine (Lamentations 4:9). Famines were the result of judgment by God (Jeremiah 14:12), general environmental changes (Ruth 1:1), pestilence (Joel 1:4–20), and military sieges (2 Kings 25). They were also used as a threat to encourage obedience (Deuteronomy 11:17). To prepare for famines, storehouses were kept full (Nehemiah 13:12) and cisterns were built to catch rainfall (Proverbs 5:15). One of the negative ramifications of famines was increasing economic inflation (2 Kings 6:24–25).

Tried, Tested, & Triumphant

The biblical story of Job is told in great detail—demanding an intensive study in order to fully understand its truth. In *Tried, Tested, & Triumphant,* Dr. Jeremiah presents the story of Job verse-by-verse, inviting you to witness every aspect of Job's challenging journey. You will not only gain a shining example to encourage you in your faith but the peace of knowing that God is in control of all things.

Thirty Amazing People in the Bible

In *Thirty Amazing People in the Bible,* Dr. Jeremiah examines thirty of his favorite biblical characters and uncovers important life lessons we can learn from their walk with God. You'll discover practical lessons and core truths to consider and apply as you study the lives of Enoch, Abraham, Joseph, Deborah, Ruth, Stephen, Philip, and more!

Turning Toward Joy

While imprisoned in Rome, Paul wrote to the Philippians of the importance of Christian joy. If Paul's relationship to Christ brought him joy even under these conditions, then surely we who also love the Savior can learn to rejoice in difficult times as well. Find out how in Dr. Jeremiah's practical study of Philippians, *Turning Toward Joy.*

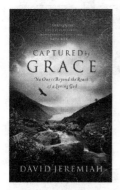

Captured by Grace

Encountering God's grace changes lives forever. Allow Dr. Jeremiah to show you how the transforming mercy that captured the apostle Paul and songwriter John Newton (author of the hymn "Amazing Grace") can awaken within you a fresh experience of the God who loves you relentlessly.

What to Do When You Don't Know What to Do

Dr. Jeremiah's line-by-line study of the book of James is for those who desire God's wisdom and intend to walk the rough road to true Christian maturity. As you study James' words, you'll gain life-changing knowledge on how to react as a believer in every kind of circumstance. And in doing so, the peace that comes from following Christ and obeying God's Word will be yours.

STAY CONNECTED
TO DR. DAVID JEREMIAH

Take advantage of two great ways to let Dr. David Jeremiah give you spiritual direction every day! Both are absolutely FREE.

Turning Points Magazine and Devotional

Receive Dr. David Jeremiah's magazine, *Turning Points* each month:

- Thematic study focus
- 48 pages of life-changing reading
- Relevant articles
- Special features
- Daily devotional readings
- Bible study resource offers
- Live event schedule
- Radio & television information

Daily Turning Point E-Devotional

Start your day off right! Find words of inspiration and spiritual motivation waiting for you on your computer every morning! Receive a daily e-devotion communication from David Jeremiah that will strengthen your walk with God and encourage you to live the authentic Christian life.

There are two easy ways to sign up for these free resources from Turning Point. Visit us online at www.DavidJeremiah.org and select "Subscribe to Daily Devotional by Email" or visit the home page and find Daily Devotional to subscribe to your monthly copy of *Turning Points*.